THE EATING AND DRINKING SERIES

"...an opinionated little compendium."
~ New York Times

"...irresistible little guide."
~ Chicago Tribune

"an elegant, small guide..."
~ Minneapolis Star Tribune

"Makes dining easy and enjoyable."
~ Toronto Sun

"...a terrific primer for first-time visitors."
~ Houston Chronicle

*"...opening up the world of good eating with their
innovative paperback series."*
~ Salt Lake Tribune

"...travelers who know their cervelle *(brains) from*
cervelle de canut *(herbed cheese spread)."*
~ USA Today

"It's written as if a friend were talking to you."
~ Celebrity Chef Tyler Florence

D1706402

ABOUT THE AUTHORS

Andy Herbach is a lawyer and resides in Palm Springs, California. He is also the author of *Eating & Drinking in Italy*, *Eating & Drinking in Spain and Portugal*, and *Eating & Drinking in Latin America*.

Andy is also the author of several travel guides, including *Paris Walks*, *The Next Time I See Paris*, *Paris Made Easy*, *French Riviera Made Easy*, *Provence Made Easy*, *Europe Made Easy*, *Amsterdam Made Easy*, *Berlin Made Easy*, *Barcelona Made Easy*, *Madrid Made Easy*, *Oslo Made Easy*, *The Amazing California Desert*, *Palm Springs Made Easy*, and *San Diego Made Easy*.

Earlier editions of this book were written with Michael Dillon. All illustrations are by Michael Dillon.

You can e-mail comments, additions and corrections to eatndrink@aol.com.

Visit our website at www.eatndrink.com

ACKNOWLEDGMENTS

French editor: Mme. Marie Fossier
English editors: Trish Medalen and Brenda McCormack
Contributors: Mark Berry, Terrie Cooper, Evelyn Coulon, Christine Humphrey, Jeff Kurz, Loralyn Lasoued, Trish Medalen, Terry Medalen, Gay Miller, Jon Miller, Jim Mortell, and Dan Schmidt

Back cover photo: Grape Gazette/Christine Humphrey

This eleventh edition has been updated by Andy Herbach. Andy thanks Karl Raaum for all his help.

Books in this series are available at special discounts for bulk purchases for promotions or premiums. Special editions, including corporate imprints and personalized covers, can be created in large quantities. For more information, contact the publisher or authors.

Eating & Drinking in

PARIS

French Menu Translator and Restaurant Guide

Andy Herbach

EUROPE MADE EASY TRAVEL GUIDES

Europe Made Easy
Travel Guides

www.eatndrink.com

Eleventh edition

Copyright © 2022 by Andy Herbach
- All Rights Reserved -

Illustrations by Michael Dillon
Updated by Andy Herbach

ISBN: 9798496286565

The authors have made every effort to be as accurate as possible,
but neither they nor the publisher assumes responsibility for the
services provided by any business listed in this guide; for any
errors or omissions; or any loss, damage, or disruptions in your
travels for any reason.

Contents

INTRODUCTION

When you think of Paris, you may think of the
Eiffel Tower, the Louvre, or the Champs-
Élysées. When we think of Paris, the first
thing that comes to mind is food.

Every traveler has a different set of desires
and expectations: rest and relaxation,
shopping, exploring, hiking, reading...
For us, the making of a memorable
vacation begins and ends with the
tastes we're going to experience.

Beyond the simple pleasures of eating, dining
in a foreign country gives you an insight into
the soul of its people. It's a glimpse of their customs, their likes and
dislikes, their heritage, their accomplishments. It puts you in contact
with local culture.

If you love to travel as much as we do, you know the importance of
a good guide. The same goes for dining in a foreign country. Why
trudge all over town, looking for a nice place to eat? A good guide
will point you in the right direction, and take the mystery out of your
next meal.

The restaurant-guide portion of our book is a list of some of our
favorite places in Paris, and the menu-translator section will help you
find your way around a menu written in French. It gives you the
freedom to fearlessly enter places you might never have entered
otherwise and order a meal.

Eating & Drinking in Paris isn't so much about food and wine. It's
really about easing the process of ordering something to eat and
having a good time – or at least not a stressful time – doing it.

Our guide was created for the traveler who wants to enjoy and experience authentic cuisine and know what he or she is eating.

ABOUT EATING AND DRINKING IN PARIS

No other city in the world has a greater number of places to eat per square mile than Paris. Nowhere else can you find the variety, the charm, the sheer joy and celebration of food. And nowhere else can you be more intimidated trying to eat. Parisians observe all kinds of decorum about their food. They have many, many types of eating establishments, which to us is confusing. They eat in a nearly ritualistic manner, and want you to do so as well. As travelers we feel we are often blundering into a private party and haven't received all the pertinent information. The following is some of that information.

THE MENU A menu is a fixed-price meal, not that piece of paper listing the food items. If you want what we consider a menu, you need to ask for *la carte*. The menu is almost always posted on the front of the restaurant so you know what you're getting into, both foodwise and pricewise, before you enter. The fixed-price daily menu (*menu fixe*) will generally include several choices for each of two or three courses. The daily fixed-price menu is cheaper than ordering off the menu (*carte*). Our American term *à la carte* means "of the menu," in case you hadn't noticed.

Restaurants frequently offer a plate of the day (*plat du jour*), and some restaurants offer a set-price tasting menu (*menu dégustation*) of specialties of the chef. The price of a meal will occasionally include the house wine (*vin compris*).

A simple green salad (*salade verte*) is occasionally served with or sometimes after the main course, before the cheese course or dessert. Rarely is this type of salad even listed on the menu. Larger, more involved – and to us what seem like full-meal – salads such as *roquefort*, *lardons*, and *endive* are usually listed as first courses or *entrées*.

An *entrée* is a first course, the *plat* is the main course, followed by cheese and then dessert. Coffee is served at the end – never with your meal. There are all sorts of coffees that you can order decaffeinated which, if your meal is ending late, as so often happens in Paris, you might want to consider. Ask for *déca*, which rhymes with day-cah. You'll find a list of the different types of coffees on page 62.

WHY IS THERE A DOG AT THE TABLE NEXT TO ME? Parisians really love their dogs. It is not uncommon (no matter what type of eating establishment you are dining in) to find several dogs under tables, or even on their own chairs.

ASKING FOR YOUR BILL The bill in a restaurant is called *l'addition*...but the bill in a bar is called *le compte* or *la note*; confusing? It's easier if you just make a scribbling motion with your fingers on the palm of your hand.

TIPPING A service charge is added by law to your bill in France. Most locals round up to the next euro and it's okay if that is what you do, too. Travelers from the U.S. sometimes have trouble *not* tipping. Remember, you do *not* have to tip. The menu will usually note that service is included (*service compris*). Sometimes this is abbreviated with the letters *s.c.* The letters *s.n.c.* stand for *service non compris*; this means that the service is not included in the price. This is *extremely* rare. If you decide to leave a tip, leave cash for the waiter. When you sign your credit card, there's rarely a space to insert a tip.

MEALTIMES In Paris, lunch is served from noon to around 2:00 p.m., and dinner from 8:00 p.m. to 11:00 p.m. Restaurants may have two seatings. Restaurants are often less crowded at the early seating, but don't worry, it most likely will fill up fast.

RESERVATIONS It's advisable if you're visiting a restaurant (as opposed to a *café*) to have reservations. Although you might see an empty restaurant and assume there will be seats available, most places we have listed will be full by 8:00 p.m. – with people who have made reservations. We advise making reservations in person. We like to do a walk-by in the afternoon, stop in and reserve a table. Don't be afraid. The word for reservation is the same in English and French. You can do times and numbers with your fingers. If you speak a little French, you can do it on the phone. The problem with phoning, however, comes when, after you've said in a timid voice that you would like to make reservations if possible, they ask you a question in rapid-fire French, and at that pace asking what your name is sounds pretty much like how many people are in the party or what time were you thinking about eating. Be patient; eventually you'll get the idea across. You can book online through the websites of many of the restaurants in this book. Some also participate in the online booking website www.thefork.com (www.thefork.fr).

WATER Europeans joke that you can tell a U.S. tourist from his "fanny pack," clothes, and ubiquitous bottle of mineral water. Tap water is safe in Paris. Occasionally, you will find *non potable* signs in restrooms. This means that the water is not safe for drinking.

Waiters and waitresses often bring *eau minérale* (mineral water) to your table. You will be charged for it, so if you don't want mineral water ask for *une carafe d'eau* or *eau du robinet* (tap water).

WHAT TO DO WHEN NOTHING SEEMS TO BE OPEN
Sundays and the month of August can be frustrating. Nothing seems to be open. You can phone in advance, but that isn't necessarily going to work because the place might not be open when you call. The best thing to do is to go to an area where there is a high concentration of restaurants. We have some of them listed on pages 14 and 15.

Closed on Sunday.

TYPES OF EATING ESTABLISHMENTS

We think of most of these places as restaurants. We have a hard time seeing the differences between many of these establishments. Cafés seem like bars, bistros seem like brasseries, and they all seem like restaurants. What some people think of as a limited menu can seem complete to someone else (like us). Our full list of restaurants starting on page 18 includes cafés, brasseries, bistros, and restaurants.

Alimentation: A small food store.
Auberge: An inn serving food and drink. These are most often found in the country, but restaurants in Paris also use the name.
Bar à café: Coffee shop serving light meals. Don't be misled by the name, though, as they rarely serve alcohol.
Bar à champagne: Champagne bar.
Bar à vin: Wine bar.
Bistro: Smaller and less fashionable than a restaurant, serving traditional, simple French food. Some are very similar to taverns or pubs.
Boucherie: Butcher's shop.
Boulangerie: Bakery. Nowhere else on earth can you get *baguettes* that taste like they do in France. Bread is often offered *bien cuit* (crusty) or *bien tendre* (doughy). Many *boulangeries* also sell sandwiches, tarts, quiches, and small pizzas.
Brasserie: Originally, this term referred to a beer hall, but today it serves food and drink.
Buffet: Eating establishment usually found in railroad stations.
Cabaret: Dinner and a show.
Café: Simple café dining is one of the pleasures of a trip to Paris. You can learn more sitting in a café for an hour than spending the day in a museum. In Paris, people-watching is like no other place in the world. Cafés serve alcoholic beverages and snacks. Some serve complete meals.
Cave: Cellar. This also refers to a wine shop. See Vins et Alcools.
Charcuterie: Originally this was a pork butcher selling pork, ham, sausages, *jambon de Paris*, and sometimes chicken. Now, most are delicatessens with prepared salads, quiches, and cured meats.
Chevaline: Horse-meat butcher's shop. These shops are becoming few and far between, but have a small and devoted clientele. Usually, there is a horse-head emblem on the front of the shop.
Chocolaterie: Chocolate shop.
Confiserie: Sweet shop.
Crèmerie: Shop with dairy products including cheese.

Crêperie: Popular for lunch, serving *crêpes* (thin filled pancakes).
Emporter: Carry-out foods.
Épicerie: Grocer's shop (literally "spice shop").
Express: Any establishment with this name is usually a snack bar.
Fromagerie: Serves up to 400 official types of cheese.
Glaces et Sorbets/Glacier: Ice cream and sorbet shop.

Berthillon
Tourists and Parisians alike line up for the best-known ice cream in the city. Over 30 flavors from *chocolat blanc* (white chocolate) to *pain d'épice* (gingerbread). It's on one of the most beautiful streets in all of Paris. *Info*: 4th/Métro Pont Marie. 29-31 rue Saint-Louis-en-l'Île (on Île Saint-Louis). Open Wed. to Sun. 10 a.m. to 8 p.m. Closed Mon., Tue., and most of Aug. Tel. 01/43.54.31.61. www.berthillon.fr

---

Hostellerie: Upscale country restaurant.
Marchand de Légumes: Vegetable shop.
Marché: Market.
Pâtisserie: Pastry shop. The Parisian favorite of *baba au rhum* (spongecake soaked in rum) was invented at **Stohrer**, 2nd/Métro Les Halles, 51 rue Montorgueil. Closed part of Aug.
Pizzeria: You can figure this one out yourself.
Poissonnerie: Seafood shop.
Relais: Country inn or restaurant.
Restaurant: See page 18 for our recommended restaurants.
Restoroute: Restaurant found on the highway.
Rôtisserie: Restaurant that usually specializes in roasted and grilled meats, especially chicken.
Salon de Thé: Open mid-morning to late evening, serving light fare, salads, cakes, ice cream, and, of course, *thé* (tea).
Tabac: Bar where you can also buy cigarettes (tabacs are, in fact, the only places in France where you can buy tobacco), stamps, tickets for public transportation, lottery tickets, and phone cards. They are often also *cafés*.
Traiteur: Delicatessen (this can also mean caterer). The food is usuacharcut
lly good and inexpensive.
Triperie: Tripe shop.
Vins et Alcools: Wine and liquor shop.
Volailler: Poultry shop.

A FEW NOTES ABOUT USING THIS GUIDE

Even people who speak passable French can have trouble reading a menu. The grand-sounding *suprême de volaille* is simply a chicken breast. *Cervelle* is brains, but *cervelle de canut* is an herbed cheese spread from Lyon.

Remember that the dish that you ordered may not be exactly as described in this guide. Every chef is (and should be) innovative. What we have listed for you in this guide is the most common version of a dish. Be careful, menus in English are often wrong.

Times can change and restaurants can close, so do a walk-by earlier in the day or the day before, if possible.

Each of our recommended restaurants offers something different. Some have great food and little ambiance. Others have great ambiance and adequate food. Still others have both. Our goal is to find restaurants that are moderately priced and enjoyable. All restaurants have been tried and tested. Not enough can be said for a friendly welcome and great service. No matter how fabulous the food is, your dining experience will always be better when you're treated well.

TIPS FOR BUDGET DINING IN PARIS

There is no need to spend a lot of money in Paris to have good food. Of course it helps when the euro is weaker than the dollar, but there are all kinds of fabulous foods to be had inexpensively all over Paris.

Eat at a neighborhood restaurant or bistro. You'll always know the price of a meal before entering, as almost all Paris restaurants post the menu and prices in the window. Never order anything whose price is not known in advance. If you see *selon grosseur* (sometimes abbreviated as s/g), this means that you are paying by weight, which can be extremely expensive.

Restaurants and bistros that have menus written in English (especially those near tourist attractions) are almost always more expensive than neighborhood restaurants and bistros.

12

Delis, *traiteurs*, and food stores can provide cheap and wonderful meals. Buy some cheese, bread, wine, and other snacks and have a picnic in one of Paris's great parks. In fact, no matter what, you should go into a *boulangerie* and buy a *baguette* at least once.

Lunch, even at the most expensive restaurants listed in this guide, always has a lower fixed price. So, have lunch as your main meal.

Large department stores frequently have supermarkets in the basement and restaurants that have reasonably priced food and wine. The ultimate grocery store (with wine cellar and carry-out) is **La Grande Épicerie** located in Le Bon Marché department store. Don't miss it! *Info*: 7th/Métro Sèvres-Babylone, 38 rue de Sèvres. Tel. 01/44.39.81.00. Open Mon. to Sat. 8:30 a.m. to 9 p.m., Sun. 10 a.m. to 8 p.m. Also at 16th/Métro La Muette, 80 rue de Passy. Tel. 01/44.14.38.00. Open Mon. to Sat. 9 a.m. to 8:30 p.m., Sun. 9 a.m. to 12:45 p.m. www.lagrandeepicerie.com.

It's also interesting to visit the supermarkets in **Monoprix**, the discount department store chain. Not at all like at home.

Street vendors generally sell inexpensive and terrific food; you'll find excellent hot dogs, *crêpes*, and roast-chicken sandwiches all over Paris. At lunch time, you'll see Parisians eating long, thin *baguettes* filled with chicken, mayonnaise, and sliced eggs throughout the city.

And, for the cost of a cup of coffee or a drink, you can linger at a café and watch the world pass by for as long as you want. It's one of Paris's greatest bargains.

FOOD MARKETS AND OTHER PLACES TO FIND FOOD

It's absolutely worth a trip to see a real outdoor Parisian market. Filled with colorful vendors, stinky cheese, fresh produce, poultry, and hanging rabbits, this is real Paris at its most diverse and beautiful. Parisians still shop (some every day) at food markets around the city. Unless noted otherwise, all are open Tuesday through Sunday. Some of the best-known are:

Rue Montorgueil, 2nd/Métro Etienne Marcel or Sentier
Rue Mouffetard, 5th/Métro Censier-Daubenton
Rue de Buci, 6th/Métro Mabillon or Odéon
Rue Cler, 7th/Métro École Militaire
Marché Bastille on the boulevard Richard Lenoir,
     11th/Métro Bastille (open Thursday and Sunday)
Rue Daguerre, 14th/Métro Denfert-Rochereau
Rue Poncelet, 17th/Métro Ternes

Organic markets are found on page 43.

There are other places around Paris where you can also see and experience food in a unique setting. The area around the Place de la Madeleine (8th/Métro Madeleine) is packed with fabulous specialty food shops, wine dealers, restaurants, and tea rooms. This is a perfect place for eating and purchasing culinary souvenirs. There is something for every taste.

In addition to food markets and specialty shops, there are several areas in Paris where many restaurants are concentrated in small pockets.

One area is on **rue Pot-de-Fer** between rue Tournefort and rue Mouffetard, just off the market. It's a slip of a street but it's lined with charming restaurants with tables set for dinner, colored lights hanging from the roof overhangs, and a uniquely Parisian ambiance (5th/Métro Monge).

There are several restaurants and bars on the lovely **Place Sainte-Catherine** (enter from rue Caron off rue Saint-Antoine) in the Marais. The Place Sainte-Catherine is a special, quiet respite in this fashionable area (4th/Métro Saint-Paul).

The colorful **Passage Brady** is in the 10th arrondissement. You can enter the narrow *passage* around 33 boulevard Strasbourg and find Indian, Turkish, and Moroccan restaurants. These are inexpensive restaurants in a working-class neighborhood (10th/Métro Château d'Eau).

You'll find loads of touristy restaurants **off rue Saint-Jacques** in the area around rue Saint-Séverin and rue de la Huchette in the 5th. This area, a short walk from Notre-Dame, is filled with French, Italian, Greek, and other restaurants jammed into small streets. It's a very pleasant walk, and you're bound to find somewhere to eat. Nearby in the 6th is the **cour du Commerce**, a tiny alleyway off rue Saint-André-des-Arts, which is lined with restaurants to fit all pocketbooks (5th/Métro Saint-Michel, Odéon or Cluny-La Sorbonne).

Climbing into the base of Montmartre, the **rue des Martyrs** is an absolute must for food lovers. Among the fabulous shops you'll find here are:

#9 La Chambre aux Confitures, jam
www.lachambreauxconfitures.com
#19 Artisan de la Truffe, truffles and products featuring the fungi
www.artisandelatruffeparis.com
#22 Sébastien Gaudard, chocolates and pastries
www.sebastiengaudard.com
#24 Henri Le Roux, chocolates
www.chocolatleroux.eu
#39 Arnaud Delmontel, bakery
www.arnaud-delmontel.com
#53/55 Collection T, French tea
www.collection-T.com
#54 Glaces Glazed, ice cream and sorbet
www.glaces-glazed.com
(9th/Métro Notre-Dame de Lorette).
Map p. 124 #22

SIMPLE RULES
FOR DINING IN PARIS

1. Just because you're a tourist, you don't have to eat like one. Looking for a place to eat while sightseeing? Here's a hint: If the menu is posted in English, there's a good chance the restaurant caters to tourists…which not only means that you'll probably be overcharged; you'll also miss out on an authentic French dining experience. This guide will help you discover where the locals eat.

2. Don't ever call the waiter "*garçon*." Though sometimes in bars a Parisian will use this word, travelers should never use it. It means "boy" and is disrespectful.

When asked what the French think about Thanksgiving Julia Child replied, "The French aren't thinking about Thanksgiving, they're focused on themselves." Which pretty much sums it up.

3. Try to make reservations. This isn't as difficult as it seems; the words are similar in both languages and they'll get the gist of what you're trying to do. We often do a walk-by in the afternoon and stop in to make the reservation. Online reservations through the websites of the restaurants makes this much easier.

Often someone/websites taking reservations will use "military"/24-hour time when asking when you want to schedule your reservation.

Return to a restaurant if you like it. If you have the luxury of time and can withstand the temptation to try other restaurants, you will always be treated better if they recognize you. Few travelers return to the same restaurant.

4. Parisians dine leisurely. Don't expect to get the same speed of service as at home. For the French, dinner is nearly a ritual.

In its full-blown form, dinner begins with an *apéritif*. This is often accompanied by an *amuse-gueule*, a little snack of some sort. After this, you order an *hors-d'oeuvre*. Then comes an *entrée*, which is a first course – *pâté* or a salad.

The main course is sometimes accompanied by or followed by a salad, but it is a simple green salad. After this, just when you think you're going to explode and have secretly unbuckled your belt, the *serveur* arrives with selections from the cheese platter that are followed by dessert, and, finally, coffee.

The server isn't intentionally ignoring you when he or she doesn't come with the bill – in France they typically don't rush you out and won't bring the bill until you ask them to.

5. Don't talk loudly. You will notice that the French speak softly, Americans don't; we just can't help it. But believe us: Those loud voices coupled with running shoes, backpacks, "fanny packs," large, conspicuous guide books, and cameras are like wearing a neon sign announcing that you are a tourist, an American tourist. There's nothing wrong with being an American tourist, but just make an attempt to behave like the French.

6. Visit a street vendor at least once in Paris. Whether it's sandwiches, hot dogs, or *crêpes*, Parisian street vendors sell delicious "food on the run." Do yourself a favor, and sample some.

7. Always be courteous. Remember that you are a guest in their country. There are simple things that the French do that we don't, like excusing yourself or saying please all the time.

Saying *s'il vous plaît* (seel voo play) after nearly everything is a safe way to be very polite. Seriously. A polite Parisian ALWAYS finishes a greeting (such as *bonjour* – hello) or affirmation (such as *oui* – yes) with a title. Thus, *bonjour* is always *bonjour, madame* or *monsieur* and yes or no is always *oui, m'sieur* or *madame*. And just so you know, you say *bonjour*, which is essentially hello, all day and night.
Bonsoir – good evening – is reserved for leaving and after sunset, and *bonne nuit* – good night – is used only when you are actually on your way to bed.

PLACES TO EAT

Phone numbers, days closed and hours of operation often change, so it's advisable to check ahead. Restaurants in tourist areas may have different hours and days of operation during low season. Reservations are recommended for all restaurants unless noted. The telephone country code for France is 33. When calling within France you must dial the area code. The area code for Paris is 01. However, you do not use the 0 before the area code when calling France from the U.S. or Canada. Confused?

Oui m'sieur? Combien de personnes?

Here's what it looks like:

From the United States and Canada:
(011) 33 1/43.26.48.23

From within Paris:
01/43.26.48.23

Prices are for a main course and without wine.
Lunch, even at the most expensive restaurants listed below, always has a lower fixed price. Credit cards accepted unless noted.

Inexpensive: under 10 euros
Moderate: 11–20 euros
Expensive: 21–30 euros
Very Expensive: over 30 euros

L'Ange 20 *Map p. 127 #1*

Don't miss this small, intimate restaurant in the heart of the Marais near the place des Vosges. Efficient and attentive service. You can watch the chef in the open kitchen. Lively mix of tourists and Parisians enjoying reasonably priced meals. Try the excellent *agneau façon sept heures* (lamb cooked for seven hours). Unbelievable what the chef turns out in this small kitchen. *Info*: 4th/Métro Chemin Vert or Bastille. 44 rue Tournelles (at rue du Pas de la Mule). Tel. 01/49.96.58.39. Closed Mon. and Tue. www.lange20.com. Moderate.

L'Avant Goût *Map p. 125 #1*

Mix with the French in this small, crowded bistro near the place d'Italie. Consistently good cuisine and very French. Try the *epaule d'agneau* (lamb shoulder). *Info*: 13th/Métro Place d'Italie. 26 rue Bobillot (from place d'Italie, south on rue Bobillot). Tel. 01/53.80.24.00. Closed Sun., Mon., and most of Aug. www.lavantgout.com. Moderate.

Bar à Iode *Map p. 125 #2*

This small seafood restaurant has a marine-themed interior and some outdoor dining. Begin with one of the starters featuring *huîtres* (oysters) and for your main course, try the *sole meunière* (with parsley butter). For dessert, binge on the *pain perdu* (French toast) with caramel ice cream. *Info*: 5th/Métro Maubert-Mutualité or Cardinal Lemoine. 34 boulevard Saint-Germain. Tel. 01/43.29.99.21. Closed Sun. and Mon. www.baraiode.fr. Moderate-Expensive. There are also locations in the 11th/Métro Charonne. 18 rue Jean Macé. Tel. 01/40.56.08.94 and in the 16th/Métro Mirabeau. 11 bis avenue des Versailles. Tel. 01/46.51.40.84.

Au Bascou *Map p. 124 #2*

This tiny bistro serves Basque specialties. It doesn't look like much from the outside, but the food will not disappoint. Try the delicious *épaule d'agneau* (lamb shoulder) or *cabillaud poêlé* (fried cod). Known for serving *lièvre à la royale*, a complex rabbit (hare) dish. Interesting regional wine list. Too bad they're closed on weekends. *Info*: 3rd/Métro Arts et Métiers. 38 rue Réaumur (at rue Volta). Tel. 01/42.72.69.25. Closed Sat., Sun., and part of Aug. www.au-bascou.fr. Moderate.

Bistrot de L'Oulette *Map p. 127 #2*

Intimate bistro in the Marais (near the place des Vosges) featuring the specialties of Southwest France (especially *confit de canard*). Excellent chestnut soup with smoked duck breast. *Info*: 4th/Métro Bastille. 38 rue des Tournelles (near rue du Pas-de-la-Mule). Tel. 01/42.71.43.33. Closed Wed. and Sun. bistrot-de-l-oulette.fr. Moderate.

Bistrot Paul-Bert *Map p. 127 #3*

A truly neighborhood bistro experience from its traditional decor to its menu written on a blackboard. Extensive wine list. Try the *entrecôte* (rib-eye steak) and the delicious *soufflé au chocolat*. *Info*: 11th/Métro Faidherbe-Chaligny. 18 rue Paul-Bert (near rue Chanzy). Tel. 01/43.72.24.01. Closed Sun. and Aug. Moderate. There's also a wine bar, **La Cave du Paul-Bert**, at number 16. Tel. 01/58.53.50.92.

Bistrotters

You won't mind the trek to this out-of-the-way neighborhood restaurant, where you'll find friendly, English-speaking servers. Start with the *foie gras du Bistrotters* (duck liver with pineapple chutney and onion). For a main course, try the excellent *croustillant de poitrine de cochon au fenouil* (crispy pork belly with fennel). For dessert, order the *pan perdu de brioche, caramel au beurre salé* (brioche bread pudding with salted-butter caramel sauce). A great experience for 33 euros for two courses. Note that reservations can be made through their website, and must be reconfirmed by email 48 hours before. It's worth the effort. *Info*: 14th/Métro Plaisance. 9 rue Decrés. Tel. 01.45.45.58.59. Open daily. www.bistrotters.com. *From Métro take rue d'Alésia, turn right on rue Decrés (one minute, .1 miles).* Moderate-Expensive.

Bouillon République *Map p. 127 #14*

This opened as Chez Jenny in 1931. The wood panels, elaborate light fixtures, and floral carpet remain but the menu has changed. All starters are less than €10, so start with deviled eggs, oysters, or snails with herb butter. You can still order sauerkraut (left over from when this was an Alsatian restaurant) and the popular onion soup with cantal cheese. Try the beef bourguignon and down it with a bottle of Ventoux, the house wine (€11). End your meal with lemon pie. Affordable French comfort food in a fun setting. *Info*: 3rd/Métro République. 39 blvd. du Temple. Tel. 01/42.59.69.31. Open daily noon-midnight.

Bouillon Pigalle is owned by the same group. It's sleek and modern with red banquettes and wooden chairs, with an emphasis on traditional fare and low prices. *Info*: 18th/Métro Pigalle. 22 blvd. de Clichy. Tel. 01/42.59.69.31. Open daily noon-midnight. www.bouillonlesite.com.

Le Bourse et la Vie *Map p. 124 #3*
Chicago-born chef Daniel Rose has closed his famous Spring (which we loved) and spruced up this bistro. Dine on French comfort-food classics such as melt-in-the-mouth *steak frites* (steak and French fries) and *pot à feu* (stew of veal and vegetables). All meals begin with *gougère* (a cheesy bread). Try the delicious *fois gras* with artichokes. Excellent desserts. *Info*: 2nd/Métro Bourse. 12 rue Vivenne (near place de la Bourse). Tel. 01/42.60.08.83. Closed Sat. and Sun. www.labourselavie.com. Expensive.

Chardenoux *Map p. 127 #4*
This small, beautiful bistro has been in business for almost 100 years. Cyril Lignac, of television cooking-show fame, has taken over and updated its menu (and prices). The menu features such dishes as *penne aux coquillages et chipirons, crème basilic* (penne with shellfish and squid in a basil cream sauce) and a flavorful lobster roll. *Info*: 11th/Métro Charonne. 1 rue Jules-Vallès and 23 rue Chanzy. Tel. 01/43.71.49.52. Open daily. www.restaurantlechardenoux.com. Moderate-Expensive.

Chez Janou *Map p. 127 #5*
Everyone seems to be having a great time at this bistro, a few blocks from the place des Vosges. Provençal and straightforward French food (very good *entrecôte*). Decent-priced wines with an emphasis on those from Provence. Known for its selection of *pastis* (anise-flavored aperitif) and delicious bowl of *mousse au chocolat* (chocolate mousse). *Info*: 3rd/Métro Chemin Vert. 2 rue Roger-Verlomme (at rue des Tournelles). Tel. 01/42.72.28.41. Open daily. www.chezjanou.com. Moderate.

Chez Paul *Map p. 127 #6*

A favorite bistro in Paris. Never a bad meal. Try *rillettes de lapin au romarin* (rabbit seasoned with rosemary), *os à moelle* (marrow bone), and the deliciously creamy *gratin dauphinois* (potatoes with eggs, cream, and cheese). *Info*: 11th/Métro Bastille or Ledru-Rollin. 13 rue de Charonne (at rue de Lappe). Tel. 01/47.00.34.57. Open daily. www.chezpaul.com. Moderate.

Au Coin de Malte *Map p. 127 #7*

You'll feel as if you've stepped into someone's living room at this cozy and casual restaurant. The menu (14 euros) is limited to three starters, three main courses, and three desserts. Choices often include *soupe à l'oignon gratinée* (French onion soup), *lasagne maison* (house lasagna), and *cuisse de poulet* (chicken drumstick with thigh). Tasty desserts. Decent house wine sold by the carafe. The staff speaks limited English, but that's why you have this guide! *Info*: 11th/Métro Oberkampf. 21 rue Oberkampf (at 1 rue de Malte). Tel. 01/43.55.19.52. Closed Sat. and Sun. Inexpensive-Moderate.

La Fontaine de Mars *Map p. 124 #4*

Red-checked tablecloths and friendly service near the Eiffel Tower. Try the *poulet fermier aux morilles* (free-range chicken with morel mushrooms). Prices seem to have increased since the Obamas ate here. Still, highly recommended. *Info*: 7th/Métro Ecole Militaire. 129 rue Saint-Dominique (near Avenue Bosquet). Tel. 01/47.05.46.44. Open daily. www.fontainedemars.com. Moderate-Expensive.

Fulgurances *Map p. 127 #15*

This innovative restaurant is a "laboratory" for up-and-coming chefs. For a limited time, a chef gets to hone his or her culinary and management skills. The result is one of the most captivating ways to experience an evening in Paris. Dishes are created using ingredients from local markets featuring small-scale producers. The tasting menu (€68) is both inventive and fun. If you have allergies, you can notify the establishment when you make your reservation and they'll accommodate you. This is a fantastic showcase for the most promising gastronomic talents in France.

The lively and fun wine bar **Fulgurances En Face** serves small plates and is located across the street at 5 rue Alexandre Dumas. Sit at one of the communal tables and sample natural wines from small French producers. *Info*: 11th/Métro rue de Boulets. 10 rue Alexandre Dumas. Tel. 01/43.48.14.59. Open Mon.-Fri. for dinner. fulgurances.com.

Another location, **L'Entrepôt**, is at 14th/Métro Pernéty. 7 Rue Francis de Pressensé. Tel. 01/45.40.07.50. Open Wed.-Sat. noon-2:30pm and 7pm-10pm, Tue 7pm-10pm.

Frenchie Bar à Vins *Map p. 124 #5*
You can sample Chef Gregory Marchand's dishes at this wine-bar annex to his (famously difficult to get into) bistro Frenchie. The menu consists of small plates. Try *terrine de campagne* and down it with a glass of wine from the interesting wine list. To score a table, you must arrive before 6:30 p.m. *Info*: 2nd/Métro Sentier. 6 rue du Nil (between rue d'Aboukir and rue Réaumur). No reservations. No lunch. Closed Sun. www.frenchie-bav.com. Moderate.

Restaurant Frenchie is at 5 rue du Nil, Tel. 01/40.39.96.19 (reservations). Closed Sat. and Sun. Lunch Thu. and Fri. www.frenchie-ruedunil.com. Expensive.

Down the street at 9 rue du Nil is **Frenchie To Go** featuring fish and chips, pickles, smoked bacon, and a delicious reuben sandwich. No reservations. There are a few seats if you want to eat on the premises, and you can wash down your food with ginger beer. Tel. 01/42.21.96.92. Open Tue. to Sun. 11 a.m. to 10 p.m. www.frenchie-ftg.com. Inexpensive-Moderate.

Le Fumoir *Map p. 124 #6*
This bar and restaurant is located near the Louvre. It's known for its Sunday brunch, salads, happy hour, and *gâteau chocolat* (chocolate cake). There's a library in the back where you can have a drink and read (and exchange your own books for the ones in their library). *Info*: 1st/Métro Louvre-Rivoli. 6 rue de l'Amiral-de Coligny (between rue de Rivoli and the River Seine). Tel. 01/42.92.00.24. Open daily 9 a.m. to 1 a.m. Closed part of Aug. www.lefumoir.com. Moderate.

Gaspard de la Nuit *Map p. 127 #8*

This cozy restaurant is located in the Marais between the place de la Bastille and place des Vosges. Traditional French cuisine. Try the delicious *carré d'agneau en croûte d'herbs* (loin of lamb with herbs) or the *coquilles Saint-Jacques* (scallops). The menu changes frequently. Always an enjoyable experience. *Info*: 4th/Métro Bastille. 6 rue des Tournelles (near rue du Pas-de-la-Mule). Tel. 01/42.77.90.53. Open daily. www.legaspard.fr. Moderate-Expensive.

Le Hangar *Map p. 124 #7*

Nothing fancy about this bistro near the Pompidou Center and next to the Anne Frank Garden. Classic French food at reasonable prices. The menu features *soupe au potiron* (pumpkin soup), *lapereau* (rabbit), and pan-fried *foie gras*. Excellent *gâteau au chocolat* (chocolate cake). *Info*: 3rd/Métro Rambuteau. 12 impasse Berthaud (off rue Beaubourg). Tel. 01/42.74.55.44. Closed Sun., Mon., and Aug. No credit cards. Moderate.

Je Thé ... Me *Map p. 125 #3*

This attractive bistro in a century-old grocery store serves classic French fare. Start with the *foie gras de canard* (fattened duck liver). For your main course, order the *carré d'agneau rôti au thym* (roasted rack of lamb with thyme) or the *coquilles Saint-Jacques* (scallops) in a citrus sauce. Friendly service. *Info*: 15th/Métro Vaugirard. 4 rue d'Alleray (off rue de Vaugirard). Tel. 01/48.42.48.30. Closed Sun., Mon., and part of Aug. www.je-the-me.com. Moderate.

Juvenile's *Map p. 124 #8*

This unpretentious wine bar serves light meals and has a large, interesting New- and Old-World wine selection. Friendly and fun. Good selection of sherry and port. The owner, originally from Scotland, has turned over the place to his daughter and her husband. Have the *terrine de campagne* (pork and liver *pâté*) or the *soupe de céleri* (celery soup) with *moules* (mussels). *Info*: 1st/Métro Bourse. 47 rue de Richelieu (near rue des Petits Champs). Tel. 01/42.97.46.49. Closed Sun. and Mon. www.juvenileswinebar.com. Inexpensive-Moderate.

La Laiterie Sainte-Clotilde *Map p. 124 #9*
The blackboard menu features French comfort food. You'll dine (in a former milk and cheese shop) with a hip local crowd. A down-to-earth bistro in an expensive neighborhood (not too far from the Musée d'Orsay). Try the *oeufs meurette* (poached eggs in red wine sauce) or the tasty *blanquette de veau* (veal stew). *Info*: 7th/Métro Solférino. 64 rue de Bellechasse (off rue de Grenelle). Tel. 01/45.51.74.61. Closed Sat. (lunch) and Sun. www.lalaiteriesainteclotilde.fr. Moderate.

Le 52 *Map p. 124 #1*
This modern bistro with concrete floors, exposed ductwork, and wooden tables is from the same owner as the popular Le Richer in the 9th arrondissement. Located in a former butcher shop on the neighborhood's busiest shopping street, it's a great choice for a casual dinner in the 10th arrondissement. The menu is limited, with about four starters, four mains, and four desserts. Highlights include *joue de cochon* (gingered pork cheek) with butternut squash, bacon, and chestnuts; and egg yolk-and-cheese-filled ravioli. We loved the *poitrine de porc* (slow-braised pork belly). Delicious desserts, especially the pear and ginger *clafoutis* with sesame ice cream and Jamaican pepper. Arrive early for dinner to get a seat. *Info*: 10th/Métro Château d'Eau or Strasbourg-Saint-Denis. 52 rue du Faubourg Saint-Denis (at cour des Petits Écuries). Tel. 01/47.70.06.86. No reservations. Open daily. www.faubourgstdenis.com. Moderate.

Les Canailles Ménilmontant *Map p. 127 #9*
Congenial bistro with a beautiful mosaic floor in a former bakery. Highlights include *épaule de cochon* (pork shoulder), *soufflé chaud au Grand-Marnier* (Grand Marnier soufflé), and the rich *profiteroles au chocolat* (cream puffs filled with ice cream and covered in chocolate sauce). Good selection of French wines by the glass. Nice choice for lunch while visiting the nearby Père-Lachaise cemetery (the eternal home of Chopin, Proust, and Jim Morrison). *Info*: 20th/Métro Ménilmontant. 15 rue des Panoyaux (off blvd. de Ménilmontant). Tel. 01/43.58.45.45. Closed Sat. and Sun. www.les-canailles-menilmontant.com. Moderate. They also have a restaurant in Pigalle. *Info*: 9th/Métro Pigalle or Saint-Georges. 25 rue la Bruyère. Tel. 01/48.74.10.48. Closed Sat. and Sun.

Mova

This comfortable restaurant with modern decor is located in the Batignolles neighborhood in the eastern part of the 17th arrondissement. Inventive dishes like *tourte de canard* (duck pie), *cabillaud* (cod) with a lobster bisque and citron, *coquilles* (scallops) with pickled asparagus, and *cochon* (pork) in a celery and mushroom sauce, make it worth a journey to the area. Excellent desserts. Lunch from €21. Dinner: Four courses for €39/six courses for €59. *Info*: 17th/Métro Rome or Place de Clichy. 39 rue des Dames (off rue des Batignolles). Tel. 01/45.22.46.07. Closed Mon. and Sun. www.mova-paris.fr. Moderate-Expensive.

Osteria Ruggera *Map p. 124 #10*

This intimate restaurant in the increasingly hip, pedestrian Montorgueil area serves delicious Italian dishes. Try the *dégustation de 5 entrées pour 2 personnes* (five antipasti for two persons) and wash it down with a bottle of Primitivo. Excellent *gnocchi de pommes de terre avec noix et gorgonzola* (potato gnocchi with gorgonzola and walnuts). *Info*: 2nd/Métro Etienne Marcel. 35 rue Tiquetonne (off rue Montorgueil). Tel. 01/40.26.13.91. Open daily. No lunch Sun. www.osteriaruggera.fr. Moderate. The casual sister restaurant **O'scià** is located across the street at 42 rue Tiquetonne and serves pizza and pasta dishes. Tel. 01/75.77.23.18. Open daily. No lunch Sun. www.pizzeriaoscia.fr.

Parcelles *Map p. 124 #11*

You'll find this intimate bistro and wine bar on a backstreet in the Marais. The chalkboard menu changes regularly and features dishes like zucchini fritters, braised beef cheek, and stuffed cabbage. It's known for its wine list with selections from small producers. If you're looking for a relaxing dining experience in the Marais, you've found your place. *Info*: 3rd/Métro Arts-et-Métiers. 13 rue Chapon (between rue du Temple and rue Beaubourg). Tel. 01/43.37.91.64. Closed Sun. www.parcelles-paris.fr. Moderate-Expensive.

Les Papilles *Map p. 125 #4*

Near the Panthéon, *Les Papilles* (Tastebuds) sells gourmet foods and wine, and offers creative takes on French cuisine. Try the tender hanger steak. Especially interesting is the *thon roti aux 4 épices et sesame grille* (tuna roasted with four spices and grilled sesame). Worth the trip! *Info*: 5th/Métro Cluny-La Sorbonne (RER Luxembourg). 30 rue Gay-Lussac (near rue Saint-Jacques). Tel. 01/43.25.20.79. Closed Sun., Mon. and part of Aug. www.lespapillesparis.fr. Moderate.

Le Petit Marché *Map p. 127 #10*
This corner café/restaurant, located on a small street off the place des Vosges, is not for those who want a quiet, romantic dinner. It's busy, noisy, and jam-packed (don't come here if you don't like to be seated in cramped quarters). The staff is helpful and most speak English. Start with the Chinese salad (*salade chinois*) or the *ceviche*. You'll find French cuisine with Asian influences such as fresh tuna tartar (*thon cru*) with toasted sesame seeds served with a Thai sauce. Main courses are served with small bowls of mashed potatoes and green beans (*haricots verts*). Other recommended dishes include the cod (*cabillaud*), lamb (*agneau*), *steak tartare* with Asian spices, and the succulent duck breast (*magret de canard*) in a honey sauce. Try the excellent raspberry (*framboise*) dessert. *Info*: 3rd/Métro Chemin Vert. 9 rue Béarn (at rue des Minimes). Tel. 01/42.72.06.67. Open daily. www.lepetitmarche.eu. Moderate.

Le Petit Prince de Paris *Map p. 125 #5*
Walk through the velvet curtains and enter the intimate dining room at this funky, fun, and friendly bistro near the Sorbonne. There are several *prix-fixe* (fixed-price) menus. Try the *magret de canard* (breast of fattened duck). Vegetarians will enjoy the *plat végétarien* (a delicious assortment of warm and cold vegetables). Fantastic chocolate desserts. *Info*: 5th/Métro Maubert-Mutualité. 12 rue de Lanneau (near rue des Ecoles). Tel. 01/43.54.77.26. Open daily for dinner. www.lepetitprincedeparis.fr. Moderate.

Au Petit Riche *Map p. 124 #12*
This classic bistro, with authentic 1880s decor, serves specialties of the Loire Valley with a Parisian twist. Try the *vol-au-vent de ris de veau* (puff pastry filled with veal sweetbreads). Very popular with tourists. *Info*: 9th/Métro Le Peletier or Richelieu-Drouot. 25 rue Le Peletier (at rue Rossini). Tel. 01/47.70.68.68. Open daily. www.restaurant-aupetitriche.com. Moderate-Expensive.

Le Potager du Père Thierry *Map p. 126 #3*

You'll receive a warm welcome at this tiny, noisy 26-seat restaurant on a touristy street in Montmartre, where you'll feel you stumbled into a fun party. Start with the excellent *oeufs en cocotte foie gras* (duck foie gras mixed with an egg). For a main course, try the *coquilles* (scallops) or the duck *confit* with mashed potatoes. For dessert, don't miss the tasty white chocolate *mousse* with raspberries. This is good rustic food, and you won't be disappointed. *Info*: 18th/ Métro Anvers. 16 rue des Trois Frères. Tel. 01/53.28.26.20. Closed Sun. Moderate.

Quedubon

Join locals at this wine bar, wine shop, and bistro located near the Parc des Buttes-Chaumont. You'll choose from a list of organic wines from the ever-changing chalkboard. Loved the free-range chicken with braised endive. Excellent and large platter of *charcuterie*. *Info*: 19th/Métro Buttes Chaumont. 22 Rue du Plateau (off rue Botzaris). Tel. 01/42.38.18.65. Closed Sat. and Sun. www.restaurantquedubon.fr. Moderate-Expensive.

Le Richer *Map p. 124 #13*

This attractive café, bar, and restaurant with exposed stone walls serves breakfast, lunch, and dinner. Try the tender *suprême de volaille* (chicken breast) or *onglet de veau, carrottes, girolles jus à estragon* (veal steak with carrots and chanterelle mushrooms in a tarragon sauce). Pleasant service. *Info*: 9th/Métro Poissonnière or Bonne Nouvelle. 2 rue Richer (near rue du Faubourg Poissonnière). Tel. 09/67.29.18.42. No reservations. Open daily. www.lericher.com. Moderate.

Le Reminet *Map p. 125 #6*

This quaint bistro is located in the Latin Quarter near place Saint-Michel and just across the river from Notre-Dame. Helpful staff and the romantic atmosphere (down to candelabras on the tables) make for a wonderful evening. Start with a *kir royale* (an aperitif made with champagne and *creme de cassis*). Try the *piccatta de veau* (veal piccatta) or *pot-au-feu* (a stew of meat and vegetables). Good wine list featuring wines from all French regions. *Info*: 5th/Métro Maubert-Mutualité or Saint-Michel. 3 rue des Grands-Degrés (one block south of Quai de la Tournelle at rue Mâitre-Albert). Tel. 01/44.07.04.24. Open daily. www.lereminet.fr. Moderate-Expensive.

These restaurants are very expensive and highly praised. Reservations well in advance are a must, as are jacket and tie.

L'Ambroisie *Map p. 125 A*
4th/Métro Saint-Paul
9 place des Vosges
Tel. 01/42.78.51.45
www.ambroisie-paris.com

Arpège *Map p. 125 B*
7th/Métro Varenne
84 rue de Varenne
Tel. 01/47.05.09.06
www.alain-passard.com

L'Atelier de Joël Robuchon
 Map p. 125 C
7th/Métro Rue du Bac
5 rue de Montalembert
(in Hôtel du Pont Royal)
Tel. 01/42.22.56.56
atelier-robuchon-saint-germain.com

Le Cinq *Map p. 124 A*
8th/Métro George V
31 avenue George V
(in the Four Seasons George V)
Tel. 01/49.52.71.54
www.fourseasons.com/paris/dining/

Epicure *Map p. 124 B*
8th/Métro Miromesnil
112 rue du Faubourg
Saint-Honoré
(in the Hotel Le Bristol)
Tel. 01/53.43.43.40
www.lebristolparis.com

Le Grand Véfour *Map p. 124 C*
1st/Métro Palais-Royal/
Musée du Louvre
17 rue de Beaujolais
Tel. 01/42.96.56.27
www.grand-vefour.com

Guy Savoy *Map p. 124 D*
6th/Métro Pont Neuf
11 Quai de Conti
Tel. 01/43.80.40.61
www.guysavoy.com

Jules Verne *Map p. 124 E*
7th/Métro Bir-Hakeim
Second level of the Eiffel Tower
Tel. 01/83.77.34.34
www.lejulesverne-paris.com

Lucas Carton *Map p. 124 F*
8th/Métro Madeleine
9 place de la Madeleine
Tel. 01/42.65.22.90
www.lucascarton.com

Pierre Gagnaire *Map p. 124 G*
8th/Métro George V
6 rue Balzac
(in Hôtel Balzac)
Tel. 01/44.35.18.00
www.hotelbalzac.com

Taillevent *Map p. 124 H*
8th/Métro George V
15 rue Lamennais
Tel. 01/44.95.15.00
www.taillevent.com

La Tour d'Argent *Map p. 125 D*
5th/Métro Maubert-Mutualité
15-17 quai de la Tournelle
Tel. 01/43.54.23.31
www.latourdargent.com

Restaurant de la Tour *Map p. 125 #7*

You'll be welcomed by the owners to the lovely dining room with Provençal décor where you'll dine on classic French fare. Try the delicious *sanglier* (wild boar) or the *ris de veau aux morilles* (veal sweetbreads with morel mushrooms). After dinner, head to the brilliantly lit Eiffel Tower, just a few blocks away. *Info*: 15th/Métro Dupleix. 6 rue Desaix (near av. de Suffren). Tel. 01/43.06.04.24. Closed Sat., Sun., and Aug. www.restaurant-delatour.fr. Moderate-Expensive.

Sacrée Fleur *Map p. 126 #4*

Meat, meat, and more meat! This welcoming restaurant near Sacré-Coeur in Montmartre is truly a find. Excellent *filet de boeuf*. Fish, veal, and pork dishes are also available. If you love rich chocolate desserts, you must end your meal with the fantastic *moelleux au chocolat* (lava cake)! Solid wine list, too. *Info*: 18th/Métro Château Rouge or Anvers. *From Métro Château Rouge go west on rue Poulet and take a right onto rue de Clignancourt*. 50 rue de Clignancourt. Tel. 01/42.51.66.18. Closed Sat. lunch and Sun. www.sacreefleur.fr. Moderate.

Sorza *Map p. 125 #8*

This small, modern Italian restaurant with stark red-and-black decor is located on the lovely Île Saint-Louis. Try the *filet de volaille aux morilles et fetuccine* (chicken fillet with morels and fetuccine) and end with the sinfully rich *mousse au chocolat* (chocolate mousse). *Info*: 4th/Métro Pont Marie. 51 rue Saint-Louis-en-l' Île (on the Île Saint-Louis). Tel. 01/43.54.78.62. Open daily. Facebook: Sorza Restaurant. Moderate.

La Veraison *Map p. 125 #9*

This casual restaurant is a real find. You'll see the chef cooking as you walk in. The food is a modern take on traditional French cooking. And it's fun to go off the beaten path. You'll be served innovative dishes such as *raviole de foie gras* (foie gras ravioli) and *magret de canard, potimarron, et poires* (duck breast with pumpkin and pears). Don't miss the *quenelles de chocolat noir à la glace caramel beurre salé* (chocolate dessert with salted caramel ice cream). *Info*: 15th/Métro Commerce. 64 rue de la Croix Nivert (at rue du Théâtre). Tel. 01/85.15.26.89. Closed Sun. and Mon. No lunch. www.laveraison.fr. Moderate-Expensive.

Historic Restaurants

Recognized the world over for its food traditions, Paris is filled with restaurants and bistros — many of which have survived and flourished for over one hundred years. Make a point of dining in at least one of these historic settings to experience the culinary heritage of this great city.

Bofinger *Map p. 127 #11*
Beautiful glass-roofed brasserie with lots of stained glass and brass, located between the place des Vosges and the place de la Bastille. It's the oldest Alsatian brasserie in Paris, and still serves traditional dishes like *choucroute* (sauerkraut) and large platters of shellfish. *Info*: 4th/Métro Bastille. 5 rue de la Bastille. Tel. 01/42.72.87.82. Open daily. www.bofingerparis.com. Expensive.

Bouillon Julien *Map p. 124 #14*
This incredibly beautiful Art Nouveau restaurant opened in 1906 and was renovated in 2018. There's a stunning stained glass ceiling, mahogany bar, and panels decorated with peacocks. Traditional dishes served include *cuisse de lapin aux olives* (leg and thigh of rabbit served in an olive sauce), *filet de dorade* (sea bream), and *pot au feu* (stew of meat and vegetables). Side dishes include everything from French fries to *petits pois* (peas). Desserts include *crème caramel* and *mousse au chocolat*. Truly an interesting experience. *Info*: 10th/Métro Strasbourg-Saint-Denis or Bonne Nouvelle. 16 rue du Faubourg Saint-Denis. 01/47.70.12.06. Open daily 11:45 a.m. to midnight. Online booking is recommended at www.bouillon-julien.com. Inexpensive-Moderate.

Bouillon Racine *Map p. 125 #10*
Brasserie in a historic building with beautiful Art Nouveau decor. Try one of the soups offered, such as *velouté de châtaignes* (cream of chestnut). *Info*: 6th/Métro Cluny-La Sorbonne or Odéon. 3 rue Racine (near blvd. Saint-Michel). Tel. 01/44.32.15.60. Open daily. www.bouillon-racine.com. Moderate-Expensive.

Brasserie Balzar *Map p. 125 #11*

This Latin Quarter brasserie opened in 1898 and serves traditional French cuisine. It's known for its *poulet rôti* (roast chicken), onion soup, and "colorful" waiters. *Info*: 5th/Métro Cluny-La Sorbonne. 49 rue des Écoles (near blvd. Saint-Michel). Tel. 01/43.54.13.67. Open daily. www.brasseriebalzar.com. Moderate-Expensive.

Brasserie Floderer *Map p. 124 #15*

Alsatian food and Parisian atmosphere at this 1886 brasserie, on a passageway in an area not frequented by tourists. Jam-packed with some of the strangest people you'll see in Paris, and getting there is half the fun. Try the *gigot d'agneau* (leg of lamb). *Info*: 10th/Métro Château d'Eau. 7 cour des Petites-Écuries (enter from 63 rue du Faubourg Saint-Denis). Tel. 01/47.70.13.59. Open daily. www.floderer-paris.com. Expensive.

Chartier *Map p. 124 #16*

In 1855, a Parisian butcher made a simple dish of *bouillon* with a slab of meat for local workers. This idea resulted in affordable restaurants named "*bouillons*," which served traditional French dishes. By the end of the 1800s, there were over 250 *bouillons* in Paris. Most were large dining rooms similar to cafeterias in the U.S. Most closed, but a few remained open, including Chartier. The *tripes à la mode de Caen* is a frequent special of the day (we passed on that). Lots of tourists, and you may be seated with strangers. Expect to wait in line. You're coming here for the experience (and the gorgeous Belle Époque dining room), not necessarily for the food. *Info*: 9th/Métro Grands Boulevards. 7 rue du Faubourg Montmartre (off blvd. Poissonnière). Tel. 01/47.70.86.29. Open daily 11:30 a.m. to 11:00 p.m. www.bouillon-chartier.com. Inexpensive.

Chez Marianne *Map p. 124 #17*

Popular take-away deli (you can also eat here, but it's difficult to get a table) known for its authentic Jewish and Eastern Mediterranean specialties, especially *falafel*. Located in the heart of the Marais. *Info*: 4th/Métro Saint-Paul. 2 rue des Hospitalières Saint-Gervais (at rue des Rosiers). Tel. 01/42.72.18.86. Open daily. www.chezmarianne.fr. Inexpensive.

La Closerie des Lilas *Map p. 125 #12*

Lenin and Trotsky are among those who have visited this historic café. There's a terrace, piano bar, brasserie (moderate), and restaurant (expensive). The brasserie is known for its *steak tartare*. *Info*: 14th/Métro Raspail or Vavin. 171 boulevard du Montparnasse (near blvd. Saint-Michel). Tel. 01/40.51.34.50. Open daily. www.closeriedeslilas.fr. Moderate-Expensive.

La Coupole *Map p. 125 #13*

A Montparnasse institution since the days of Picasso, this noisy brasserie known for its *huîtres* (oysters) is a favorite among tourists. *Info*: 14th/Métro Vavin. 102 boulevard du Montparnasse (at rue Vavin). Tel. 01/43.20.14.20. Open daily. www.lacoupole-paris.com. Expensive.

Le Grand Colbert *Map p. 124 #18*

Housed in a restored historic building, serving traditional brasserie cuisine. Known for its seafood tray. This stunning restaurant was featured in the movie *Something's Gotta Give*, so lots of tourists. *Info*: 2nd/Métro Bourse. 2 rue Vivienne (near the Place des Victoires). Tel. 01/42.86.87.88. Closed part of Aug. www.legrandcolbert.fr. Expensive.

Aux Lyonnais *Map p. 124 #19*

This beautiful century-old bistro has been renovated and serves the cuisine of Lyon. Try the *sanglier* (wild boar) when available. The wine of choice is Beaujolais. It's part of the Alain Ducasse group. *Info*: 2nd/Métro Bourse. 32 rue Saint-Marc (off rue de Richelieu). Tel. 01/42.96.65.04. Closed Sun. dinner, Mon., and Tue. www.auxlyonnais.com. Expensive.

Ma Bourgogne *Map p. 127 #12*

Ma Bourgogne another favorite.

This café/restaurant in the place des Vosges (the oldest square in Paris) serves traditional Parisian cuisine and specializes in *poulet rôti* (roast chicken). Good salads. Open for breakfast, lunch, and dinner. *Info*: 4th/Métro Saint-Paul. 19 place des Vosges. Tel. 01/42.78.44.64. Open daily. www.ma-bourgogne.fr. Moderate.

Perraudin *Map p. 125 #14*

You'll get to know your fellow diners at this inexpensive bistro serving traditional Parisian cuisine just steps from the Panthéon. Try the *gigot d'agneau* (roasted leg of lamb) or the *boeuf bourguignon*. *Info*: 5th/Métro Cluny-La Sorbonne. 157 rue Saint-Jacques (near rue Soufflot). Tel. 01/46.33.15.75. Closed Sun. www.leperraudin.fr. Inexpensive-Moderate.

Polidor *Map p. 125 #15*

You'll sit at communal tables at this popular old-fashioned bistro serving traditional cuisine such as *pintade* (guinea hen). French comfort food. *Info*: 6th/Métro Odéon. 41 rue Monsieur-le-Prince (near rue Racine). Tel. 01/43.26.95.34. Open daily. No reservations. No credit cards. www.polidor.com. Moderate.

Terminus Nord *Map p. 124 #20*

What a great way to arrive in (or depart from) Paris! This large, bustling brasserie near the Gare du Nord is just so Parisian with its mahogany bar, polished wood, and beveled glass. Seafood platters, *bouillabaisse*, and duck breast are the featured dishes. *Info*: 10th/Métro Gare du Nord. 23 rue de Dunkerque. Tel. 01/42.85.05.15. Open daily. www.terminusnord.com. Expensive.

Le Train Bleu *Map p. 127 #13*

Forget all the food you've eaten in train stations. *Beautiful* It's delicious here. The setting, with its murals *Restaurant!* of the French-speaking world, is spectacular. A great place to have a drink. *Info*: 12th/Métro Gare de Lyon. 20 boulevard Diderot (in the Gare de Lyon train station). Tel. 01/43.43.09.06. Open daily. www.le-train-bleu.com. Expensive.

Willi's Wine Bar *Map p. 124 #21*

Since 1980, the British owners of this attractive wine bar have been serving specialties with Mediterranean influences. A great wine list, and a favorite of many travelers to Paris. *Info*: 1st/Métro Bourse. 13 rue des Petits-Champs (near rue Vivienne). Tel. 01/42.61.05.09. Closed Sun. and part of Aug. www.williswinebar.com. Moderate-Expensive.

PLACES TO DRINK

More wine bars are listed above in the Places to Eat section.

L'Art Source

This attractive wine bar with stone walls and beamed ceiling is located on a pedestrian street off rue Montorgueil. The helpful English-speaking staff will guide you through the wines by the glass. Small plates offered include mini-burgers and *ceviche*. In warm weather, there's a small and comfortable area in front where you can sit outside. Great choice for a late-night drink and snack. *Info*: 2nd/ Métro Etienne Marcel. 6 rue Marie Stuart (off rue Montorgueil). Tel. 09/82.55.00.49. Open Tue. to Sat. at 6:30 p.m. www.lartsource.fr. Inexpensive-Moderate.

Le Baron Rouge

Have a glass of wine (some right from the barrel) at this neighborhood wine bar. You'll sit at communal tables. Try the *charcuterie*, cheese platters, and oysters (on weekends). It's especially busy on Sunday afternoons. *Info*: 12th/Métro Ledru-Rollin. 1 rue Théophile Roussel. Tel. 01/43.43.14.32. Closed Sun. dinner and Mon. lunch. No reservations. www.lebaronrouge.net. Moderate.

Café de la Nouvelle Mairie

This bustling wine bar/café near the Panthéon serves classic French food and small plates. There are about twenty wines served by the glass (starting at €4) and many are organic. Especially nice in the summer. English-speaking staff. Always packed elbow-to-elbow. *Info*: 5th/Métro Cardinal Lemoine or RER B Luxembourg. 19 rue des Fossés Saint Jacques. Tel. 01/44.07.04.41. Closed most weekends. Inexpensive-Moderate.

Coinstot Vino

Guillaume Dupré runs this casual wine bar located in the passage des Panoramas, the oldest *passage* in Paris. In addition to the superior wine list, you can order small plates (such as wild bass on endive) or select from a few main courses. *Info*: 2nd/Métro Grands Boulevards. 22-30 Galerie Montmartre. Tel. 01/44.82.08.54. Closed Sat. lunch, Sun., Mon. (dinner), and part of Aug. coinstotvino.business.site. Moderate.

Le Dokhan's

An elegant champagne bar where you can enjoy it
by the flute or by the bottle. Try the three champagnes
for €30. *Info*: 16th/Métro Trocadéro. 117 rue Lauriston
(in Hôtel Le Dokhan's). Tel. 01/53.65.66.99. Open daily
6 p.m. to midnight. www.marriott.com.

Coupe de Champagne.

Le Garde Robe

This wine bar near the Louvre features mostly organic wines (with an
emphasis on white wines from the Loire) and has a knowledgeable
staff. Delicious *charcuterie* and cheese plates. *Info*: 1st/Métro Louvre-
Rivoli. 41 rue de l'Arbre Sec. Tel. 01/49.26.90.60. Closed Sat. (lunch)
and Sun. Moderate.

Au Lapin Agile

You'll hear French folk tunes at this shuttered cottage at the picturesque intersection of rue des Saules and rue Saint-Vincent. It was
once frequented by Picasso. You'll sit at small wooden tables and lis-
ten to *chansonniers* (singers). Truly a Parisian experience. *Info*: 18th/
Métro Lamarck-Caulaincourt. 22 rue des Saules. Tel. 01/46.06.85.87.
Open Tue. to Sun. 9 p.m. to 1 a.m. Closed Mon. Admission: €35
(includes a drink). No credit cards. Reservations can be made at
au-lapin-agile.com. *Map p. 126 #2*

Le Trésor

Cocktails and bistro fare served both inside and outside at tables
along this lovely, flowered street in the heart of the Marais. Great
people-watching. *Info*: 4th/Métro Hôtel de Ville or Saint-Paul. 5-7
rue du Trésor (off rue Vieille du Temple). Tel. 01/42.71.35.17. Open
daily. www.restaurantletresor.com. Moderate.

En Vrac

The name means "in bulk" and you can have bottles (with stoppers)
filled with your choice of wines to go. At €4 to €8 a bottle, that's
quite a deal. The bar is lined with wine-filled steel tanks. There's a
plat du jour along with cheese plates, *charcuterie*, and sandwiches
made to order. *Info*: 18th/Métro Marx Dormoy. 2 rue de l'Olive
(at the corner of 92 rue Riquet). Tel. 01/53.26.03.94. Open Mon.
to Sat. 10 a.m. to 9 p.m., Sun. 10 a.m. to 3 p.m. www.vinenvrac.fr.
Inexpensive.

FOOD AND WINE SHOPS

Bakeries (Boulangeries), Chocolate Shops (Chocolateries), Pastry Shops (Pâtisseries), and Candy Stores (Confiseries)

Kayser

Excellent *baguettes*, specialty breads like the coarse and hearty *pain au levain*, and delicious *pain au chocolat*. *Info*: 5th/Métro Maubert-Mutualité. 8 and 14 rue Monge (other locations throughout the city). 8 rue Monge: Tel. 01/44.07.01.42. Open daily. 14 rue Monge: Tel. 01/43.54.95.19. Closed Mon. and Tue. www.maison-kayser.com.

Lenôtre

Elegant café and restaurant. Especially known for their pastries. Lenôtre has several shops in Paris. *Info*: 16th/Métro Victor Hugo. 48 avenue Victor Hugo. Tel. 01/42.02.21.21. Open daily 9 a.m. to 8 p.m. Closed part of Aug. www.lenotre.com.

La Maison du Chocolat

A French "luxury" chocolate maker. Every chocolate lover should visit. There are several shops in the city, including 8 boulevard de la Madeleine (9th/Métro Madeleine). Tel. 01/47.42.86.52 and 225 rue du Faubourg Saint-Honoré (8th/Métro Ternes). Tel. 01/42.27.39.44. Closed Sun. www.lamaisonduchocolat.fr.

Patrick Roger

Patrick Roger's attractive shop on the boulevard Saint-Germain has excellent chocolates packaged in green boxes that make great gifts and are easy to pack to take home. *Info*: 6th/Métro Odéon. 108 boulevard Saint-Germain. Tel. 01/43.29.38.42. Open daily. Other locations include 16th/Métro Kleber. 45 avenue Victor Hugo. Tel. 01/45.01.66.71. Closed Sun. www.patrickroger.com.

Stohrer

The Parisian favorite *baba au rhum* (spongecake soaked in rum) was invented at this *pâtisserie* in the Montorgueil quarter. *Info*: 2nd/Métro Les Halles. 51 rue Montorgueil. Tel. 01/42.33.38.20. Open daily. Closed part of Aug. www.stohrer.fr.

À La Mère de Famille

The oldest *confiserie* in Paris (since 1761). Gorgeous store! Locations throughout the city. *Info*: 9th/Métro Le Peletier or Cadet. 35 rue du Faubourg Montmartre. Tel. 01/47.70.83.69. Open daily. Closed part of Aug. www.lameredefamille.com.

Cheese Shops (Fromageries)

Alléosse

Cheese is like gold to the French. Charles de Gaulle is reported to have said, "How can anyone govern a nation that has 246 different kinds of cheese?" This cheese shop on a busy market street serves rare cheeses from throughout France. *Info*: 17th/Métro Ternes. 13 rue Poncelet. Tel. 01/46.22.50.45. Closed Sun. afternoon and Mon. www.fromage-alleosse.com.

Barthélemy

This small cheese shop on the Left Bank is where Parisians shop for their cheese. When you walk in, you're overtaken by the intense smell of some of the best cheeses available in France. *Info*: 7th/Métro Rue du Bac. 51 rue de Grenelle. Tel. 01/42.22.82.24. Closed Sun., Mon., and Aug.

Taka & Vermo

This modern cheese shop features selections from small producers throughout France and Europe. Try the brie stuffed with candied chestnuts and the truffled cheese (with black truffles from the Périgord region). There's an on-site *cave* for *affinage* (cheese ripening and aging) that allows the young cheesemakers to be creative. *Info*: 10th/Métro Strasbourg-Saint-Denis. 61 bis rue du Faubourg Saint-Denis. Tel. 01/48.24.89.29. Closed Mon. takavermo.fr.

Specialty Food Stores (Épiceries)

Boutique Maille
Boutique mustard shop on the place de la Madeleine. *Info*: 8th/Métro Madeleine. 6 place de la Madeleine. Tel. 01/40.15.06.00. Closed Sun. www.maille.com.

Lafayette Gourmet
This department store has a huge gourmet-food section, with tasting bars, restaurants, and deli counters. *Info*: 9th/Métro Chaussée d'Antin. 35/40 boulevard Hausmann (in the Galeries Lafayette department store). Tel. 01/40.23.52.67. www.galerieslafayette.com.

La Grande Épicerie
The *ultimate* grocery store (with wine cellar and carry-out). Don't miss it! *Info*: 7th/Métro Sèvres-Babylone. 38 rue Sèvres (in Le Bon Marché department store). Tel. 01/44.39.81.00. Open daily. www.lagrandeepicerie.com. A second location is at 16th/Métro La Muette, 80 rue Passy. Tel. 01/44.14.38.00. Open daily.

G. Detou and **A. Simon**
You'll find a little of everything food-related at this shop near the rue Montorgueil (one of the best fish and meat markets in the city). Great gifts to take home include dried mushrooms, chocolates, olive oil, glazed chestnuts, and canned *foie gras*. *Info*: 2nd/Métro Etienne Marcel. 58 rue Tiquetonne. Tel. 01/42.36.54.67. Closed Sun. You can also visit their incredible kitchenware shop **A. Simon** nearby at 48 and 52 rue Montmartre. Tel. 01/42.33.71.65. Closed Sun.

La Maison du Miel
This food store offers everything made from honey (from sweets to soap). *Info*: 9th/Métro Madeleine or Opéra. 24 rue Vignon. Tel. 01/47.42.26.70. Closed Sun. www.maisondumiel.fr.

La Dernière Goutte

Located in an old vaulted room.
The owners are charming and
friendly, and they frequently have
wine tastings in English. The name
of the shop means "the last drop."
Info: 6th/Métro Saint-Germain-des-Prés. 6 rue de Bourbon-le-
Château (at rue de l'Echaudé). Tel. 01/43.29.11.62. www.ldgparis.
com.

Les Caves Taillevent

This wine shop is associated with the well-known Taillevent res-
taurant and is said to have over 500,000 bottles of wine. You'll be
amazed at the cost of some selections. *Info*: 8th/Métro Charles de
Gaulle-Étoile or Saint-Philippe-du-Roule. 228 rue du Faubourg
Saint-Honoré. Tel. 01/45.61.14.09. Open 10 a.m. to 7:30 p.m.
Closed Sun. and most of Aug. www.lescavesdetaillevent.com.

Lavinia

One of the largest wine shops in Paris, with foreign wines, French
wines, and spirits, priced from 4 to 4000 euros. There's a restaurant
here where you can order *charcuterie* (with wine from the shop, of
course). *Info*: 16th/Métro Victor Hugo. 22 ave. Victor Hugo. Tel.
01/42.97.20.20. Open Tue. to Sat. 11 a.m. to 8 p.m. Closed Sun. and
Mon. www.lavinia.fr.

Legrand Filles et Fils

In the elegant and beautiful Galerie Vivienne, you'll find luxurious
stores and this wine bar and shop. It's been run by the Legrand family for over three generations. Sandwiches, salads, and cheese platters
are offered here. A great place for a light lunch. Be sure to check out
the cork-covered ceiling. The galerie leads into the Galerie Colbert,
a glass-domed arcade built in 1823. *Info*: 2nd/Métro Bourse. 1 rue
de la Banque. Tel. 01/42.60.07.12. Open Mon. to Sat. 10 a.m. to
7:30 p.m. Closed Sun. and part of Aug. www.caves-legrand.com.

Ô Chateau

"Coming to Paris and not tasting good French wines is like going to the U.S. and not trying a good burger," says Olivier Magny, the French sommelier and proprietor of Ô Chateau. Magny, who speaks fluent English (he spent time in California after graduating from business school), started wine tastings from a small venue in Paris before moving to this location, just a five-minute walk from the Louvre. He and his international staff will guide you through a fun, informative, and relaxing wine tasting. Ô Chateau's wine bar, the largest in Paris, offers over 40 wines by the glass, and over 100 wines by the bottle. If you arrive before 7 p.m., you likely won't need a reservation. And if you want something to enjoy with your wine, order one of their excellent cheese platters. In addition to the wine bar, there are three private rooms – with beautiful vaulted ceilings and wine-filled shelves – for tastings and special events. Check out their website for wine tastings (from €59). Among the offerings are a wine and cheese lunch (€75 – including five glasses of wine) and a wine tasting dinner (€99 – including four glasses of premium wine). *Info*: 1st/Métro Louvre-Rivoli. 68 rue Jean-Jacques Rousseau. Tel. 01/44.73.97.80. Closed Sun. www.o-chateau.com.

La Cave Des Papilles

This wine store, with a bright yellow facade, has been in operation for over 20 years. Located in the 14th arrondissement, it's known for its large selection of natural wines. 80% of the wines offered here are produced organically by small French wine growers. *Info*: 14th/Métro Gaîté or Denfert-Rochereau. 35 rue Daguerre. Tel. 01/43.20.05.74. Open daily. lacavedespapilles.com.

Nicolas

A good selection of French wines, champagnes, and spirits are found at these wine stores. One is most likely around the corner from where you are staying as there are nearly 200 Nicolas stores located throughout Paris. *Info*: www.nicolas.com.

Tearooms (Salons de Thé)

Ladurée

Elegant *salon de thé* and pastry shop
on the charming rue Cler. Try a *maca-*
ron. There are many other locations
throughout the city. *Info*: 7th/Métro La Tour-Maubourg. 47 rue Cler.
Tel. 01/44.26.36.69. Open daily. www.laduree.fr.

Dammann Frères

Are you a teetotaler? This tea shop is located on the place des
Vosges. Walk in and you will find yourself surrounded by walls
lined with shelves holding black canisters filled with rare teas,
which you can sample before you purchase. The elegant boxes make
great gifts or souvenirs. *Info*: 4th/Métro Saint-Paul or Bastille. 15
place des Vosges. Tel. 01/44.54.04.88. Open daily.
www.dammann.fr.

Mariage Frères

400 types of teas offered in
elegant rooms serving light meals
and weekend brunch. *Info*: 6th/
Métro Odéon or Saint-Michel.
13 rue des Grands Augustins
(other locations throughout the
city). Tel. 01/40.51.82.50. Closed
Sun. www.mariagefreres.com.

Organic, Vegan, Vegetarian, Gluten-Free, and Lactose-Free

Paris is embracing the organic food movement. There are several
grocery stores featuring organic products:
BioCoop, throughout Paris, including 5th/Métro Cardinal Lemoine,
17 rue Monge and 11th/Métro Bréguet-Sabin, 10 rue Boulle. Closed
Sun. www.biocoop.fr.

Naturalia, throughout Paris, including 4th/Métro Hôtel de Ville, 11
rue Renard and 5th/Métro Cardinal Lemoine, 36 rue Monge. Closed
most Sun. www.naturalia.fr.

There are also several organic outdoor markets, including:
Marché bio Raspail, boulevard Raspail, 6th/Métro Rennes (Sun. morning)
Marché bio Brancusi, place Brancusi, 14th/Métro Gaîté (Sat. morning)
Marché bio Batignolles, boulevard des Batignolles, 17th/Métro Place de Clichy (Sat. morning)

Le Grenier de Notre-Dame

This vegetarian/vegan restaurant is located on a quiet street near the Seine River and Notre-Dame. Try the vegetarian *cassoulet* (bean casserole). *Info*: 5th/Métro Saint-Michel. 18 rue de la Bûcherie (between rue Lagrande and rue de l'Hôtel Colbert). Tel. 01/43.29.98.29. Open daily. www.legrenierdenotredame.fr. Moderate.

Noglu

This gluten-free restaurant (and take-out) also offers some lactose-free dishes. The menu changes daily and features everything from *cabaillaud* (cod) to pizza. Excellent desserts. Saturday brunch. *Info*: 11th/Métro Voltaire. 15 rue Basfroi. Tel. 01/42.36.52.50. Open daily. There's also a location at 7th/Métro Rue du Bac. 69 rue de Grenelle. Tel. 01/58.90.18.12. Open daily. www.noglu.fr. Moderate.

Soya

You'll find inventive vegetarian and vegan dishes at this small, intimate restaurant. Try the lasagna stuffed with tofu. Excellent list of organic wines. *Info*: 11th/Métro République. 20 rue de la Pierre Levée (off rue de la Fontaine-au-Roi). Tel. 01/48.06.33.02. Closed Sun. dinner. www.soya-cantine-bio.fr. Moderate.

Le Potager du Marais

This small vegetarian/vegan restaurant is in the Marais. Try the *soupe à l'oignon gratinée* (French onion soup). *Info*: 4th/Métro Saint-Paul. 26 rue Saint-Paul. Tel. 01/57.40.98.57. Closed Mon. and Tue. www.lepotagerdumarais.fr. Moderate.

CAFÉS

Café Beaubourg

Looking onto the Centre Pompidou
and packed with an artsy crowd.
We meet friends here every year
and always have a great time!
Info: 4th/Métro Rambuteau. 43 rue
Saint-Merri. Tel. 01/48.87.63.96.
Open daily 9 a.m. to 1 a.m. www.
cafebeaubourg.com.

Café Les Deux Magots

If you're a tourist, you'll fit right in at one of Hemingway's favorite
spots. We don't really recommend that you eat here (there is a limited menu), but have a drink and enjoy the great people-watching.
Info: 6th/Métro Saint-Germain-des-Prés. 6 place Saint-Germain-des-
Prés. Tel. 01/45.48.55.25. Open daily 7:30 a.m. to 1 a.m.
www.lesdeuxmagots.fr.

Café de Flore

Another famous café and a favorite of tourists and Parisians alike
(next door to Les Deux Magots). *Info*: 6th/Métro Saint-Germain-
des-Prés. 172 boulevard Saint-Germain-des-Prés.
Tel. 01/45.48.55.26. Open daily 7:30 a.m. to 1:30 a.m.
www.cafedeflore.fr.

Café de l'Industrie

Near the Opéra Bastille, this inexpensive café features a limited
menu, a diverse wine list, and an interesting crowd. *Info*: 11th/Métro
Bastille. 16 rue Saint-Sabin. Tel. 01/47.00.13.53. Open daily 9 a.m.
to 2 a.m. www.cafedelindustrieparis.fr.

Café Joyeaux

Among the fast food chains, expensive tearooms, and overpriced
restaurants on the Champs-Élysées is this café near the Arc de
Triomphe. The delicious food and desserts found here are served by
people with disabilities. All of the profits go toward opening other
cafés with the same mission. *Info*: 8th/Métro George V or Charles

de Gaulle – Étoile. 144 Champs-Élysées. Tel. 01/44.07.12.63. Open Mon.-Sat. 8:30 a.m.-9:30.p.m. Also at 2nd/Métro Quatre Septembre. 23 rue Saint-Augustin. Tel. 01/42.21.02.78. Open Mon. 10:30 a.m. to 3 p.m., Tue.-Sat. 10:30 a.m. to 7:30 p.m. www.cafejoyeux.com.

Café L'Été en Pente Douce
Interesting and picturesque Montmartre café near Sacré-Coeur. Take a break here after you climb the steps to Sacré-Coeur! *Info*: 18th/Métro Château Rouge or

L'été en pente douce ~ Summer on a gentle slope.

Anvers. 8 rue Paul Albert/23 rue Muller. Tel. 01/42.64.02.67. Open daily noon to midnight. If you're facing Sacré-Coeur, take the steps down to your right (rue Maurice-Utrillo) and at the bottom is rue Muller and the café. lete-en-pente-douce.business.site. *Map p. 126 #1*

Café de la Paix
Famous café (not really known for its food). Popular with tourists. Another spot for outdoor people-watching (and the inside is stunning). *Info*: 9th/Métro Opéra. 5 place de l'Opéra. Tel. 01/40.07.36.36. Open daily 8 a.m. to 11 p.m. (Fri. and Sat. until 11:30 p.m.). www.cafedelapaix.fr.

Café Marly
This café overlooks the pyramid at the Louvre and no place in Paris has a better setting. Standard bistro fare served by waiters in suits. It's a great place for a relaxing lunch, or come here after dinner and end your day with a glass of champagne.

We love the pyramids.

Definitely worth the cost! You can also view the Eiffel Tower in the distance. *Info*: 1st/Métro Palais-Royal/Musée du Louvre. 93 rue de Rivoli. Tel. 01/49.26.06.60. Open daily 8 a.m. to 1.a.m. www.cafe-marly.com.

French Pronunciation Guide

If you're looking for a comprehensive guide to speaking French, this is not the right place. What follows are simply a few tips for speaking French and a very brief pronunciation resource.

It is always good to learn a few polite terms so that you can excuse yourself when you've stepped on the foot of an elderly lady or spilled your drink down the back of the gentleman in front of you. It's also just common courtesy to greet the people you meet in your hotel, shops and restaurants in their own language.

If a word ends in a consonant and that word is followed by a word that starts with a vowel, the consonant is linked to the vowel. So, *vous avez* (you have) is pronounced voozavay. And the final consonant in a word is silent (unless followed by an e).

a like in far

e like in open

é and ez like the a in rate

è like the e in bet

ê like eh as in *crêpe*

i like the i in machine

o like the o in not

ô like the o in wrote

u round your lips as to say oh, but say ee

an, am, en, em, ant, ent like the a in wand

au, eau like the o in okay

er at the end of a word sounds like the ay in day

in, im, ain, aim like the a in sank

ou like the oo in cool

oi like the wa in water

que like the cu in curve

qui like kee

un is pronounced uhn

c like a k before a, o, u, and consonants

c like an s before e and i

ch like sh

ç like the s in simple

g before a, o and u, like in good

g like the s in pleasure before i and e

gn like the ny in canyon

h is always silent

j like the s in measure

r like an r being swallowed

s like the s in step but, when between vowels, it's pronounced like a z

ss like an s

zh like the s in measure

ENGLISH-TO-FRENCH WORDS AND PHRASES

This is a brief listing of some familiar English foods and food-related words that you may need in a restaurant setting. It is followed by a list of phrases that may come in handy. There are also some pronunciation prompts. They aren't all exactly perfect, but they're close enough to get you what you need.

allergic, allergique *anchois~*
anchovies, anchois *an - sh wa*
appetizer, hors-d'oeuvre
apple, pomme
artichoke, artichaut
ashtray, cendrier
asparagus, aspèrge
bacon, lard (lardons)
baked, au four/cuit au four
banana, banane
beans, fève
beef, boeuf
beefsteak, bifteck/steak
beer, bière
beverages, boissons
bill, l'addition
bitter, amer
boiled, bouilli *bouteille~*
bottle, bouteille *boo-tay*
bottle (half), demi-bouteille
bowl, bol
braised, braisé
bread, pain
bread roll, petit pain

breakfast, petit déjeuner
broth, consommé
butter, beurre
cabbage, chou
cake, gâteau
candle, chandelle/bougie
carrot, carotte
cereal, céréale(s)
chair, chaise
check, l'addition
cheers, santé
cheese, fromage
cherry, cerise
chicken, poulet
chicken breast, suprême de volaille
chops, côtelettes, côtes
clams, palourdes
cocktail, cocktail
cod, morue
coffee, café
coffee (American-style), café américain
coffee w/milk, café crème/un crème (*café au lait* if you want a lot of milk)
coffee (black), café noir
coffee (decaf), déca/décafféiné
cold, froid
corn, maïs
cover charge, couvert
credit card, carte de crédit
cucumber, concombre
cup, tasse
custard, crème anglaise
dessert, dessert
dinner, dîner

dish (plate), assiette. A main
    dish is *plat principal*

drink, boisson

duck, canard

eggs, oeufs

espresso, café express/un
    express

fish, poisson

fish soup, bouillabaisse (the
    famous seafood stew)

fork, fourchette

french fries, frites (pommes
    frites)

fresh, fraîche/frais

fried, frit

fruit, fruits

game, gibier

garlic, ail *ail ~*

gin, gin *aye*

glass, verre

goat, chèvre

goose, oie

grapefruit, pamplemousse

grapes, raisin

green beans, haricots verts

grilled, grillé

ham (cooked), jambon (cuit)

ham (cured), jambon (de
    Parme and de Bayonne)

hamburger, hamburger

honey, miel *Chaud ~*

hot, chaud *Froid*

ice, glaçon *SHoW ~*

ice cream, glace *FwA*

ice (on the rocks), avec des
    glaçons

ice water, l'eau glacée

included, compris

ketchup, ketchup

knife, couteau *Couteau - coo·toe*

kosher, casher/kascher

lamb, agneau

large, grand

lemon, citron

lettuce, laitue

little, petit/peu de...

liver, foie

lobster, homard

loin, longe (pork)/aloyau (beef)

lunch, déjeuner *déjeuner ~ day-juh-nay*

match, allumette

mayonnaise, mayonnaise

meat, viande

medium (cooked), à point

melon, melon

menu, carte

milk, lait
    Lait écrémé is skim milk
    and *lait entier*, whole milk

mineral water, eau minérale

mineral water (sparkling),
    eau minérale (gazeuse)

mineral water (w/out carbonation), eau minérale plate (non
    gazeuse)

mixed, mélange, mixte,
    mesclun (salad greens)

mushrooms, champignons

mussels, moules

mustard, moutarde

napkin, serviette

noodles, pâtes/nouilles

nuts, noix

octopus, poulpes

oil, huile
olive oil, huile d'olive
olives, olives
omelette, omelette
on the rocks (w/ ice), avec des
  glaçons
onions, oignons *Oignons ~*
orange, orange *ON-yone*
orange juice, jus d'orange
overdone, trop cuit *huîtres ~*
oysters, huîtres *weeT-RAH*
partridge, perdrix
pastry, pâtisserie
peaches, pêches
pears, poires
peas, petits pois
pepper (black), poivre
peppers (sweet), poivrons
perch, perche
pineapple, ananas
plate (dish), assiette
please, s'il vous plaît
plums, prunes
poached, poché
pork, porc
potatoes, pommes de terre
poultry, volaille
prawns, grosses crevettes/
  langoustines
quail, caille
rabbit, lapin
rare, saignant
raspberry, framboises
receipt, note/reçu
rice, riz
roast, rôti
rolls, petits pains

salad, salade
salmon, saumon
salt, sel
sandwich, sandwich(e)
sauce, sauce
sautéed, sauté
scallops, coquilles (Saint-
  Jacques) *brouille~*
scrambled, brouillé *brew-ee*
seafood, fruits de mer
seasonings, condiments/
  assaisonnement
shellfish, crustacés
shrimp, crevettes
small, petit
smoked, fumé
snails, escargots
sole, sole
soup, soupe
spaghetti, spaghetti
sparkling (wine), champagne
specialty, spécialité *epice ~*
spicy, épicé *AY-PEE-SAY*
spinach, épinards
spoon, cuiller/cuillère
squid, calmar/calamar
steak, steak/bifteck
steamed, vapeur
stew, ragoût
strawberries, fraises
sugar, sucre
sugar substitute, édulcorant/de
l'aspartam
supper, dîner
sweet, doux/sucré
table, table
tea, thé

tea w/lemon, thé citron
tea w/milk, thé au lait
thank you, merci
tip, pourboire
toast, pain grillé   *grillé ~ gree-AY*
tomato, tomate
toothpick, cure-dents
trout, truite
tuna, thon
turkey, dindon/dinde
utensil, couvert
veal, veau
vegetable, légume
vegetarian, végétarien
venison, venaison
vinegar, vinaigre
vodka, vodka
waiter, monsieur (never
    garçon)
waitress, madame or
    mademoiselle
water, eau
watermelon, pastèque
well done, bien cuit. Very well
    done is *très bien cuit*
whipped cream, crème
    chantilly *(shan-tee-ee)*
wine, vin
wine list, carte des vins
wine (red), vin rouge
wine (rosé), vin rosé
wine (white), vin blanc
with, avec
without, sans
yogurt, yaourt

HELPFUL PHRASES

please, s'il vous plaît
thank you, merci
yes, oui
no, non
good morning, bonjour
good afternoon, bonjour
good evening, bonsoir
good night, bonne nuit
goodbye, au revoir

Do you speak English?,
    parlez-vous anglais?
I don't speak French,
    je ne parle pas français
excuse me, pardon
I don't understand,
    je ne comprends pas
I'd like a table,
    je voudrais une table
I'd like to reserve a table,
    je voudrais réserver une table
for one person,
    pour une personne *-UNE*
for two, pour deux *_ deh*
--trois (3)   *-Twa*
--quatre (4)   *- CaT*
--cinq (5)   *- Sank*
--six (6)   *- see*
--sept (7)   *- seT*
--huit (8)   *- weeT*
--neuf (9)   *- nurf*
--dix (10)   *- deece*

this evening, ce soir
tomorrow, demain
near the window, près de la fenêtre
with a view, avec vue
outside on the patio, sur la terrasse
no smoking, non-fumeur. Since January 2008,
    smoking is banned in all restaurants
where is?, où est
where are?, où sont
the bathrooms, les toilettes
the bill, l'addition
a mistake (error), une erreur
Is service included?, Le service est-il compris?
Do you accept credit cards?, acceptez-vous les cartes de crédit
traveler's checks, chèques de voyage
How much is it?, c'est combien?
What is this?, qu'est-ce que c'est?
I did not order this, ce n'est pas ce que j'ai commandé
This is, c'est
--too, trop *— Trow*
--cold, froid *— FWA*
--hot, chaud *— SHow*
--not fresh, n'est pas frais *— NAY PAH FRAIS*
--rare, saignant *— SANE-YANT*
--undercooked, pas assez cuit *— PAH AHSAY CWEE*
--overcooked, trop cuit *TROW CWEE*
--delicious, délicieux
I am a vegeterian, Je suis végétarien(ne)
without meat, pas de viande/sans viande
closed, fermé
Monday, lundi *Lundee*
Tuesday, mardi *Mardee*
Wednesday, mercredi *Mare KRA dee*
Thursday, jeudi *Juh dee*
Friday, vendredi *Yawndradee*
Saturday, samedi *Samahdee*
Sunday, dimanche *Dee mansh*

MENU TRANSLATOR

AAAAA, the seal of approval of
*l'Association Amicale des Amateurs
d'Andouillettes Authentiques.*
Only in France would they have an
association for devotees of
andouillette (tripe sausage)

*In French
Amateur means
"Lover of"*

abats, abattis, organ meats

abricot, apricot

acras/accras, *beignets,* usually stuffed
w/seafood, found in the French West Indies

acidulé, acidic

addition (l'addition), check/bill

affinée, aged

agneau, lamb

agneau de lait, milk-fed lamb

agneau pré-salé, lamb grazed on salt marshes

agrumes, citrus fruits

Agrumes.

aiglefin, haddock

aïgo bouido, garlic soup (means "boiled water")

aigre, sour

aigre-doux, sweet and sour

aigrelette, a sour sauce

aiguebelle, herbal after-dinner drink similar to *Chartreuse*

aiguillette, thin slice. *Aiguillette de boeuf* are slices of steak

ail, garlic

aile, wing of poultry

aile de raie, ray fin (a kite-shaped
fish also called skate)

*Aile is used
to mean
white meat.*

aile et cuisse, *aile*: literally wing,
it means white meat in fowl
cuisse: literally leg, it means dark meat in fowl

ailerons, wings

aillade, garlic mayonnaise (see *aïoli*)

aillade gasconne, veal w/garlic found in Southwest France

aïoli/ailloli, garlic mayonnaise. Found in many
provençal dishes

aïoli garni, *aïoli* served w/boiled food, salt cod, vegetables and eggs

airelle, cranberry

à la, à l', au, aux, in the manner of, in, with

à la carte, side dishes (each item ordered separately)

albert, a sauce of egg yolk, cream, horseradish, shallots and mustard

albuféra, *béchamel* sauce w/sweet peppers

alcool, alcohol

algues, seaweed

ali baba, spongecake soaked in rum

aligot, garlic mashed potatoes w/cheese

alimentation, food/food store

allumettes, puff pastry or potato strips

alose, shad (fish)

alouette, lark

alouette sans tête, rolled veal slice
   stuffed w/garlic and minced meat

aloyau, sirloin

Alsace, located in the northeast corner of France (along the
   German border); one of France's wine regions specializing
   in white wines such as Gewürztraminer, Riesling, Pinot Gris,
   Pinot Blanc, Pinot Noir and Sylvaner

alsacienne, alsacien/usually garnished w/sausage and sauerkraut
   (means "Alsace style")

amande, almond

amande de mer, small shellfish

amandine, w/almonds

amer/amère, bitter

américaine, white wine sauce usually w/brandy,
   shallots, tomatoes and garlic w/shrimp/lobster

Amer Picon, aperitif (wine and brandy w/herbs)

amidon, starch. *Amidon de blé* is cornstarch

amourettes, the bone marrow of an ox or calf

amuse-bouche, appetizer

amuse-gueule, appetizer

ananas, pineapple

anchoïade, anchovy spread from Provence

anchois, anchovy

ancienne, "old style": usually means a
   wine cream sauce w/mushrooms,
   shallots or onions

andalouse, usually w/eggplant, tomatoes
   and green peppers

[handwritten note:] Alouettes Sans têtes ~ Larks without heads!

[handwritten note:] Bouche ~ mouth
gueule ~ throat
These are small morsels of food
Just a mouthful or two.

andouille, tripe sausage

andouillette, small tripe sausage

aneth, dill

angélique, the crystallized stalks of the herb angelica (a decoration for cakes)

anglaise, boiled/boiled or steamed vegetables/breaded, fried meat, fish or vegetables

We have a general rule about tripe: Don't. But we love andouillette.

anguille, eel. Many dishes in the French West Indies feature eels

anguille au vert, eel in a white sauce w/parsley

anis, aniseed

apéritif, drink before dinner

à point, medium rare

appellation d`origine contrôlée, an officially recognized wine of France. Sometimes designated by A.O.C. The makers of A.O.C. are the best of the French wine industry

arachide, peanut

araignée de mer, spider crab

ardennaise, usually means served w/berries ("Ardennes style")

ardoise, specials are often written on the *ardoise*, a chalk board. This can also mean (for regular customers) that they put it on your running bill

arête, fish bone

argenteuil, asparagus soup

arlequin, two flavors

armagnac, brandy (similar to *cognac*). The main difference is *cognac* is distilled twice (and thus smoother) while *armagnac* is distilled only once

armoricaine, in a tomato sauce

arôme, aroma

aromates, herbs and spices

aromatisé, flavored

artichaut, artichoke

artichauts à la barigoule, artichokes w/mushrooms and pork

artichaut violet, small artichoke

asperge, asparagus

asperge à la flamande, white asparagus w/egg sauce. A Belgian specialty

asperge d'Argenteuil, large white artichoke

aspic, gelatin

aspic de volaille, chicken in aspic

assaisonnement, dressing/seasoning

assiette, plate

assiette anglaise, cold cuts

assiette de charcuterie, assorted meat products (cold cuts)

assiette de crudités, a plate of raw vegetables

assiette du pêcheur, assorted fish plate

assorti, assorted

asturienne, w/livers

au, in

aubergine, eggplant

Aubergine.

aulx, garlic (the plural of *ail*)

aumônière, *crêpe* filled and wrapped into the shape of a little
    purse. The word means "beggar's purse"

aurore, a tomato sauce

auvergnat, usually means served w/sausage and cabbage (means
    "Auvergne style")

aux, with

avec, with

avec des glaçons, on the rocks

avocat, avocado

avoine, oats

Avec des glaçons.

aziminu, Corsican *bouillabaisse*

baba au rhum, spongecake soaked in rum

bäckaoffa, meat and potato stew from Alsace

bacon, Canadian bacon

baeckeoffe, baked meat and
    potato stew from Alsace

bagna cauda, hot anchovy dip from Provence

baguette, long and thin loaf of bread

baies, berries

baigné, bathed

ballottine (de volaille), boned meat
    (poultry) stuffed, rolled,
    cooked and served in gelatin

Ballotine. Not sure about this concept.

banane, banana

bananes flambées, bananas flamed in brandy

bananes vertes, green bananas used in dishes in the
    French West Indies

Bandol, popular wine from Provence. The red is full-bodied
    and spicy and the white is fruity, often with a hint of aniseed

banon, cheese from Provence dipped in *eau-de-vie* and wrapped in chestnut leaves

bar, bass

barbarie, Barbary (a type of duck)

barbouiado, vegetable *ragoût*

barbue, brill (fish)

barde, the lard or bacon put over roasts

barigoule, artichoke hearts, sausage, bacon, garlic and mushroom dish

Barigoule. Like the sound of it

baron, the hindquarter and leg of a lamb

barquette, small boat-shaped pastry. *Une barquette* means "a carton of"

Barry, à la du, served w/a cauliflower and cheese sauce

basilic, basil

basquaise, served w/tomatoes, or red peppers ("Basque style")

bâtard, a small *baguette*

batonnets, crisp sticks. *Batonnets de courgette* are crisp zucchini sticks

baudroie, monkfish
This can also refer to a fish soup w/garlic and vegetables

bavaroise, custard dessert

bavette, flank steak

béarnaise, *hollandaise* sauce w/vinegar, tarragon, shallots and wine

Sauce Béarnaise.

béatilles, mixed organ meats

beaufort, a hard cheese

Beaujolais, one of France's wine regions (on the south tip of Burgundy) noted for fruity red wines. *Beaujolais Nouveau* is light and fruity and denotes the first wine to be released

beaumont, a mild cheese

bécasse, woodcock

bécassine, snipe

béchamel, white sauce (usually butter, milk [and/or cream] and flour)

beckenoff, pork and mutton baked w/potatoes

beignet, fritter filled w/fruit, meat and/or vegetables (a filled doughnut)

belle étoile, a mild cheese

belon, a type of oyster

bénédictine, dark green, brandy-based liqueur

Belle étoile ~ beautiful star.

bergamotte, a variety of lemon or pear

bercy, fish stock *velouté* w/white wine, shallots and parsley

berlingots, mint-flavored caramels

betterave, beet

beuchelle, creamed kidneys and sweetbreads

Betterave.

beurgoule, caramel-rice pudding

beurre, butter

beurre blanc, white butter sauce of white wine, vinegar and shallots

beurre blanc nantais, white butter and shallot sauce for fish

beurre d'ail, garlic butter

beurre d'anchois, anchovy butter

beurre de montpellier, green butter (made green from herbs)

beurre d'estragon, tarragon butter

beurre fondu, melted butter

beurre maître d'hôtel, butter w/chopped parsley and lemon juice

beurre manié, butter and flour thickening for sauces

beurre nantais, white butter

beurre noir, browned butter sauce (until it's almost black)

beurre noisette, lightly browned butter

bicard de soude, baking soda

biche, female deer

bien cuit, well done

bière, beer

bière à la pression, draft beer

bière blonde, lager beer

Bière.

bière brune, dark beer

bière légère, light beer

bifteck, beef steak

biftek de cheval, horse-meat steak

bigarade, brown sauce usually w/vinegar, sugar and oranges

bigarreau, a type of cherry

bigorneaux, small sea mollusks

bigourneau, the shellfish periwinkle

billes de melons, melon balls

billy bi, cream of mushroom soup

biscotte, zwieback (sweetened bread enriched w/eggs, baked and sliced and toasted until dry and crisp)

biscuit, biscuit/cookie
biscuit à la cuillère, ladyfingers
biscuit de Savoie, spongecake
biscuits aux brisures de chocolat,
    chocolate-chip cookies
bisque, chowder
bisque d'écrevisses, freshwater
    crayfish chowder
bisque de homard, lobster bisque
bisque de langoustines, saltwater
    crayfish chowder

Bisque de ...
ecrevisses, homard,
Langoustines ...
Love 'em all.

blaff, spicy stewed fresh fish
    dish served in the
    French West Indies
blanc, white
blanc-cassis, white wine and
    black currant liqueur
blanc de blancs, white wine made from white grapes
blanc de poireau, the white part of a leek
blanc de volaille, boned breast of poultry
blanchaille, whitebait, a fish
blanchi, blanched
blanquette, stew
blanquette de veau, veal
    stew in a white sauce

Blanc Cassis
is a popular
aperatif
in France.

blé, wheat
blé de turquie, corn
blé dur, duram wheat
blette, Swiss chard
bleu, blue cheese/meat prepared nearly raw/fish boiled very
    fresh. Some popular blue cheeses
    are bleu d'Auvergne, bleu de Bresse,
    bleu des Causses and bleu du Haut-Jura
blini, small pancakes (usually w/sour
    cream, caviar and salmon)
blonde, light (as in light-colored
    [lager] beer)
boeuf, beef
boeuf à la ficelle, beef cooked in stock
boeuf à la gardiane, beef and wine stew w/black olives
boeuf à la gordienne, braised beef dish from Provence

boeuf à la mode, beef marinated in red wine

boeuf bourguignon, beef stewed in red wine (burgundy) w/onions, bacon and mushrooms

boeuf braisé à la beauceronne, beef casserole found around Orléans

boeuf en daube, larded chunks of beef marinated and cooked in wine/beef casserole

boeuf miroton, beef stew or boiled beef w/onion sauce

boeuf mode, beef stew w/carrots. This can also refer to cold beef in jelly

boeuf salé, corned beef

bohémienne, eggplant and tomato casserole. A specialty in Nice

boisson, beverage

boissons compris, drinks included

boissons non compris, drinks not included

boîte, can, box or jar. *Une boîte de conserve...* means a can of...

boles de picolat, meatballs and mushrooms cooked in a sauce

bolet, boletus mushroom

bombe/bombe glacée, layered ice cream

bon, bonne, good

bonbons, candy

bonne femme, homestyle cooking. *Bonne femme means Good Woman.* This can also refer to a *sauce veloutée* w/*crème fraîche* and lemon juice

bonnefoy, *sauce velouté* w/shallots and white wine

Bordeaux, one of France's wine regions (the largest wine-producing area in the world). Red *Bordeaux* is made from a blend of cabernet sauvignon, merlot, cabernet franc, malbec and petite verdot grapes. White *Bordeaux* is made from semillon and sauvignon blanc grapes.

bordelaise, red wine sauce w/mushrooms, beef marrow and shallots

botte, bunch (as in a bunch of herbs). *Botte de radis* means bunch of radishes

bouchée, bite size. *Cidre bouché* refers to alcoholic, dry cider

bouchée à la reine, puff pastry filled w/meat, seafood, sweet breads and/or mushrooms

boucherie, butcher shop. *Boucheries chevalines* are still found in France and are horse-meat butcher shops

bouchon, cork

boudin, blood sausage (black pudding)

boudin blanc, white sausage
(sausage of white meats)
boudin liège, Belgian sausage
boudin noir (boudin antillais), spicy
blood sausage (a specialty
in the French West Indies)
bougon, a goat's milk cheese
bouillabaisse, shellfish and fish stewed
in white wine, olive oil, saffron,
tomatoes and garlic. There are many versions of this dish
bouilli, boiled/boiled beef
bouillon, broth/stock
boulanger, baker. *Boulangère* is a woman baker
boulangerie, bakery
boule de fromage frit, fried cheese ball
boulette, meatball or fishball
boulette de semoule, semolina and potato *gnocchi*
boulghour, bulgur wheat
boullinade, thick soup found in the South of France
bouquet, large (red) shrimp (usually served cold)
bouquet garni, a small bundle of herbs
and/or spices tied together in
cheesecloth and used to provide
flavor to dishes while they cook
bouquet rose, prawns
bourbon, bourbon
bourboulhade, salt cod and garlic soup.
Sometimes referred to as
a poor man's *bouillabaisse*
bourdaines, apples baked in pastry
bourdaloue, butter cake w/fruit
Bourgogne, Burgundy. Burgundy is one of France's wine
regions (famous for red wines made from pinot noir grapes)
Bourgueil, light, fruity wine from the Loire Valley
bourguignon/bourguignonne, mushrooms and onions in a red
wine sauce (see *boeuf bourguignon*)
bouribut, red wine duck stew
bourride, a fish stew found in the South of France (thickened
w/egg yolks and *aïoli*)
boursin, a mild, soft cheese
boutargue, smoked fish roe

Boudin is also an unflattering term for a woman.

Bouquet garni can be found in boxes packaged like tea bags and are great.

bouteille, bottle
braisé, braised
braiser, to braise
branches de céleri, celery stalks
brandade, cod and potato dish
brandade de morue, salt cod w/garlic,
    cream and olive oil
brandy, brandy
brebis, sheep's-milk cheese
brème, bream
Bretagne, Brittany, an Atlantic coastal province
bretonne, usually a dish served w/white wine sauce or white
    beans ("Brittany style"). This can also refer to a type of
    oyster
brézzolles, slices of veal
bricks, round, paper-thin sheets of pastry (usually filled w/egg
    and Middle Eastern spices). A specialty of Tunisia
brie, white, mellow, soft cheese. If you don't know what *brie* is,
    you shouldn't be in France
brins, branches or sprigs
brioche, small sweet cake or roll
broccio, a cheese (similar to *ricotta*) found in Corsica
broche, (on a) spit
brochet, pike
brochette de coeurs, heart kabob. A specialty in Toulouse
brochette, en, cooked on a skewer
brocoli, broccoli
broufado, braised beef w/anchovies
brouillade d'aubergines, stuffed eggplant w/tomatoes
brouillé, scrambled
Brouilly, red wine from Beaujolais
brousse de brebis, soft and mild sheep's- or goat's-milk cheese
brousse du Rove, cheese (similar to *ricotta*) made w/sheep's
    milk. The sheep graze on
    thyme, which gives the cheese
    its unusual flavor
brugnon, nectarine
brûlé, burned/caramelized
brune, dark (as in dark beer)
brunoise, diced vegetables
brut, very dry

Bouteille ~
Bootay

Brins de romarin.

Brugnon.

bûche de Noël, rolled Christmas cake
buffet froid, a variety of cold dishes
bugnes, fried doughnuts
buisson, vegetable dish
bulot, large sea snail
Burgundy, a wine (red, white or rosé) produced in the
    Burgundy region
Byrrh, sweet wine (fortified w/brandy) mixed w/quinine
cabécou, a strong, round goat cheese
Cabernet Sauvignon, dry red wine
cabillaud, cod
cabri, kid goat
cacahuète, peanut
cacao, cocoa
cachat, fresh cheese from Provence
Caen, à la mode de, cooked w/*calvados*
café, coffee (really, espresso)
café américain, American-style coffee
café au lait, coffee w/milk
café brûlot, flaming coffee
    (strong coffee w/liquor
    which is set on fire)
café complet, continental breakfast
    (coffee, bread, butter and jam)
café crème, coffee w/cream
café déca, decaffeinated coffee
café décaféiné, decaffeinated coffee
café de Paris, the name for a butter
    sauce flavored w/cognac and herbs
café espresso, espresso
café express, espresso
café filtre, drip-brewed coffee/
    American-style coffee
café frappé, iced coffee
café glacé, coffee-flavored ice
    cream/iced coffee
café liégeois, cold coffee
    served w/ice cream
café nature, black coffee
café noir, black coffee
café sans caféine, decaffeinated coffee

Bûche de Noël.

Café américain.

If you want to order American coffee without seeming so... American, you can order Café élongée. (AY-Lon-jay) It's just French coffee "elongated" with water.

café soluble, instant coffee
café viennois, coffee w/whipped cream
cagouille, small land snail
caille, quail
caillete, pâté of pork, herbs and garlic
calalou, "pepperpot" stew w/many
    ingredients found in the French West Indies
calamar, squid
calissons, marzipan candies
    shaped like boats from Aix
calmar, squid
calvados, apple brandy
camembert, soft cheese w/strong flavor
camomille, camomile tea
campagne, à la, this term means "country style" and has many
    different meanings
canapé, appetizer w/bread base and topped w/various ingredients
canard, duck
canard à la presse, roast duck dish w/red wine and Cognac
canard à l'orange, roast duck braised w/orange sauce
canard de Barbarie, a duck breed in Southwest France
canard de Challans, a type of small duck
canard de Nantes, a type of small duck
canard de Rouen, a type of wild duck
canard laqué, Peking duck
canard Montmorency, duck w/cherries
canard rôti, roast duck
canard sauvage, wild duck
cancoillotte, strong, hard cheese (melted before serving) from
    the Franche-Comté region in Eastern France
candi, candied
caneton, duckling
canette, young female duck
canistrelli, dry cookies from Corsica
cannelle, cinnamon
cantal, a cheese very much like cheddar
caouanne, turtle
capoun fassum, cabbage stuffed w/rice and sausage
câpre, caper
caqhuse, pork and onion casserole
carafe, carafe

caramélisé, caramelized

caramel, burned sugar. This also refers to a chewy vanilla or chocolate caramel

carapaces, shells

carbonnade, braised beef stew (a Belgian specialty) also charcoal-grilled meat

Carapaces refers to shrimp or Lobster Shells.

carbonnade à la boeuf, Belgian specialty of beef marinated in beer and cooked in onions and herbs

carbonnade bruxelloise, Belgian dish of pork w/a tomato and tarragon sauce

carbonnade flamande, beef, herbs and onions braised in beer

carbonnade nîmoise, lamb and potato dish

cardinal, fish stock *velouté*, lobster, butter and cream

cardamome, cardamom

cardon, cardoon (a member of the thistle family)

cargolade, grilled snail dish from Languedoc-Roussillon

cari, curry

carotte, carrot

carottes glacées, carrots glazed in butter

carottes râpées, grated carrots

carottes Vichy, steamed carrots (in butter and parsley)

carpe, carp

carré, rack/loin/fillet

carré d'agneau, rack or loin of lamb

carré de l'Est, pungent cheese (square shaped)

carré de porc, rack or loin of pork

carré de veau, rack or loin of veal

carrelet, flounder/plaice

carte, la, menu

carte des vins, wine list

carvi, caraway seeds

casse-croûte, snack ("breaking the crust")

The French are not so much for snacking, casse-croute refers to a small-meal type snack.

casse-pierre, seaweed

cassis, black currant/black currant liqueur

cassolette, dish served in a small casserole

cassoulet (toulousain), meat and bean (and often sausage) casserole. This dish originated in Southwest France

castagna, chestnut in Corsican

castanhet, chestnut cake

cavaillon, a fragrant melon from the town of the same name in Provence. It looks like a small cantaloupe

cave, wine shop/wine cellar

caviar, fish eggs

Celeri.

caviar d'aubergine, eggplant purée

cédrat, citron

céleri, celery

céleri-rave, celery root

céleri rémoulade, celery root in a creamy mayonnaise dressing

cendre chemisée, smoldering

cèpe, boletus mushroom

céréale, cereal

cerf, venison (deer)

cerfeuil, chervil

cerise, cherry

cerise noire, black cherry

Cerf.

cerises jubilé, cherries flamed w/*kirsch* and served w/ice cream

cerneau, the "meat" of a walnut

cervelas, seasoned sausage made from brains

cervelle, brains

cervelle de canut, herbed cheese spread

chabichou, cow's- and goat's-milk cheese. Some think it has a sweet flavor

Cervelle. Apparently Some people like it.

Chablis, one of France's wine regions producing white wine made from the chardonnay grape

chair, "fleshy" part of fish or meat

Challonaise, wine region producing mostly table wine

chambré, room temperature (when serving wine)

chamois, mountain goat

Champagne, A region in Northeastern France famous for its sparkling wines classified by the sugar content. ***Brut*** is the driest, ***extra-sec*** is very dry, ***sec*** is dry, ***demi-sec*** is slightly sweet and ***doux*** is sweet. Also a sweet cookie served w/champagne

champenoise, sparkling wine

champêtre, this term means "rustic" and can mean many things – usually it signifies a simple dish

Champignons.

champignon, mushroom

champignon à la grecque, cold mushroom appetizer

champignon de bois, wild mushroom

champignon de Paris, button mushroom

champignon de pin, pine mushroom.
A wild mushroom found in Provence

champignon sauvage, wild mushroom

changement de garniture, this means an extra charge for substitutions

chansons aux pommes, flaky breakfast pastry w/apple filling

Chansons aux pommes means Songs to apples.

chanterelle, chanterelle mushroom

chantilly, sweet whipped cream.
This can also refer to *hollandaise* sauce and whipped cream

chaource, cheese found in the Champagne region

chapelure, breadcrumbs

chapon, capon

chapon de mer, scorpion fish

charbonnade, charcoal-grilled meat

charcuterie, can be a deli or any place serving prepared salads, quiches, and cured meats.
This can also refer to a plate or platter of cured meats

charcuterie assortie, assorted cold meats

chariot, dessert and/or cheese cart

Chariot... be on the Lookout!

charlotte, fruit dessert made in a mold/baked fruit compote/pudding

charolais, denotes a high-quality beef

chartreuse, yellow (or green) herb liqueur. Also a game bird (usually pheasant or partridge) dish from Alsace

chasse, venison

chasselas, a white grape

chasseur, "hunter's style" usually means in a sauce w/tomatoes, wine, herbs and mushrooms

Chasse means hunt.

châtaigne, chestnut

châtaignes chaudes/marrons chauds, roasted chestnuts

chateaubriand, thick slice of tenderloin stuffed w/sauteed shallots and usually served w/butter or *béarnaise* sauce

Château-Margaux, red wine from Bordeaux

Châteauneuf-du-Pape, red wine from the Rhône River valley

Châteauneuf du Pape means the Pope's new castle.

chaud, hot

chaud-froid, cold poultry dish/a
dish containing gelatin. It's
cooked and then served cold, thus
the name which means "hot-cold"

chaudrée, seafood and fish stew
(contains the white part of squid)

chauffé, heated

chaumes, rich, creamy cheese from Dordogne

chausson, fruit turnover

chausson aux pommes, apple turnover

chemise, en, baked in parchment/wrapped in
pastry/potato w/the skin left on

cheval, horse

chèvre, goat/goat cheese

chevreau, young goat

chèvre fraîche, goat cheese which is only a few days old

chèvre sèche, dried (aged) goat cheese

chevreuil, deer

chichi, orange-flavored doughnuts/can also mean "fancy"

chicons du Nord, Belgian endive

chicorée, chicory/endive

chicorée frisée, curly lettuce

chicorée witloof, Belgian endive

chiffonnade, shredded leafy vegetables and herbs

chinchard, saurel, a fish

chinois, Chinese

Chinon, red wine from the Loire Valley

chipiron, small squid

chipirons en su tinta, Basque dish of squid
cooked in its own ink

chipolatas, small sausages

chips, potato chips

chivry, a *béarnaise* sauce w/spinach, parsley or watercress
added to make it green

chocolat, chocolate

chocolat à la bayonne, chocolate cream dessert

chocolat amer, bitter chocolate

chocolat au lait, milk chocolate

chocolat chaud, hot chocolate

chocolat mi-amer, bittersweet chocolate

Hot Chocolate is more common in Europe than in the U.S.

chocolat noir, bitter chocolate/black chocolate

choix, "choice." On a menu, this means you can choose among a list of dishes

chope, large beer

choron, *béarnaise* sauce w/tomatoes

chou, cabbage

chou à la crème, cream puff

choucroute, sauerkraut. In Alsace, this refers to a dish of cabbage w/pork, potatoes and sauerkraut

Love choucroute garni!

choucroute garnie, sauerkraut w/ham, pork sausage or frankfurters

chouée, buttered cabbage dish

chou-fleur, cauliflower

chou frisé, kale/savoy cabbage

chou marin, kale

chou rouge, red cabbage

Mon petit Chou is a term of endearment.

chou vert, green cabbage

choux de Bruxelles, brussels sprouts

ciboule, scallion

ciboulette, chive

cidre, cider. Popular in Brittany

cigales, a type of clam

cigarette, sugar cookie (rolled in the shape of a cigarette)

citron, the term for lemons-and limes (citrus fruit) but can also simply refer to a lemon

citronelle, lemon grass

citronnade, lemon drink

citron pressé, fresh lemon juice w/sugar and water (lemonade)

citron vert, lime

citrouille, pumpkin

civelles, baby eels

civet, game stew. Popular in Corsica

civet de lapin, rabbit stew

civet de lièvre, hare stew

clafouti, fruit baked in pancake batter

LOVE this

clafouti du limousin, cherry *clafouti*

claires, oysters (raised in an oyster bed)

clamart, stuffed w/green peas

Claret, dry, red table wine from Bordeaux

clémentine, seedless tangerine

clos, vineyard
clou de girofle, clove
clouté, "studded with"
cocaos, cocoa
cochon, pig

Cochon.

I'll pass.

cochon de lait, suckling pig
cochon de lait en gelée, suckling pig in aspic
cochonnailles, assorted pork sausages and pâtés
cocotte, casserole
coeur, heart

Cocotte.

coeur d'artichaut, artichoke heart
coeur de filet, thickest and best part of a beef filet
coeurs de palmiers, hearts of palm served w/a mustard
    vinaigrette
cognac, cognac
coing, quince
Cointreau, orange-flavored liqueur
colbert, à la, dipped in batter and breadcrumbs and fried
colin, hake
colonel, lemon sherbet w/vodka
colvert, wild duck
complet, full/whole
compote, stewed fruit
compote de..., stewed
compris, included
comté, a mild cheese (similar to the Swiss gruyère cheese)
concassé, chopped
concentré, concentrate
concombre, cucumber
concorde, chocolate meringue and chocolate mousse
condiments, seasoning
confiserie, candy and sweets shop
confit, goose, pork, turkey or duck preserved in fat.
    Also vegetables/fruit preserved in alcohol, sugar or vinegar
confiture, jam/preserves.
    Confiture d'oignons is onion compote
confiture de vieux garçon, fruit served in alcohol
confiture d' orange, marmalade
congre, conger eel
consommation, drinks
consommé, broth (clear soup)

*Vieux Garçon
means Old boy.
Something like
old maid.*

consommé aux vermicelles, broth w/thin noodles
consommé Célestine, broth w/chicken and noodles
consommé colbert, broth w/vegetables and poached eggs
consommé madrilène, cold broth w/tomatoes
consommé princesse, broth w/chicken and asparagus
consultez aussi l'ardoise, other suggestions
on the blackboard
consultez notre carte des desserts, consult our dessert menu
contre-filet, sirloin
copeaux, shavings (of vegetables or chocolate) *Coq au vin.*
copieux, filling *gotta have*
coppa, fillet (in Corsica) *it in*
coq, rooster *Paris*
coq au vin, chicken stewed in red wine
w/bacon, onions, mushrooms and herbs
coq de bruyère, grouse
coque, tiny shellfish (similar to a clam)
coquelet, cockerel
coquillage, shellfish
coquille, shell/scallop
coquille Saint-Jacques, scallops (prepared w/a *Coquille.*
parsley butter or a cream sauce)
coquilles à la nantaise, scallops w/onions.
A specialty in Brittany
corail, the egg sac of lobster,
crayfish or scallops
corbeille, basket
corbeille de fruits, basket of assorted fruits
cordon bleu, veal slices stuffed w/ham and
gruyere, breaded and fried in butter *Corbeille.*
coriandre, coriander
cornet de frites, paper cone filled
w/french fries. A popular snack
cornets de murat, cones filled w/cream
cornichon, small pickle (gherkin)
corniottes, cheese pastries made in the shape of hats
corps, refers to the "body" of wine
corsoise, à la, this means that the dish is prepared
as it would be in Corsica
cosse, pod/husk
côte, rib/chop

côte d'agneau, lamb chop

Côte de Beaune, red and white wines from Beaune in Burgundy

côte de boeuf, beef rib steak/T-bone steak

Côte de Nuits, a heavy red Burgundy wine

côte de veau, veal chop

côtelette, cutlet/chop

côtelette d'agneau, lamb chop

côtelette de porc, pork chop

Côtes du Rhône, wine region producing wines such as
   Châteauneuf-du-Pape, Côte-Rotie, Hermitage and *Tavel*

côtes levées, spareribs

cotignac, caramelized apple tart

cotriade, fish stew (from Brittany)

cou, neck

cou d'oie farci, a "sausage" made of the neck skin of a goose
   which is stuffed w/meat and spices

couennes de porc, fresh pork rinds

coulibiac, salmon *pâté*

coulis, vegetable, shellfish or fruit purée

coulis de tomates, thick tomato sauce

coulommiers, a mild cheese (similar to *brie*)

coupe, goblet/scoop/a dish used for serving dessert

coupe Danemark, a scoop of vanilla ice
   cream covered w/hot chocolate sauce

coupe de champagne, a flute of champagne   *Coupe de*

coupe des îles, a scoop of vanilla ice cream   *Champagne.*
   w/fruit and whipped cream

coupe glacée, ice cream dessert (often a sundae)

courge, squash

courgette, zucchini

courgettes au broccio, *broccio* cheese-stuffed
   zucchini dish from Corsica   *Couronne*

couronne, circle-shaped or ring-shaped bread   *means crown*

court bouillon, seafood broth   *or wreath.*

couscous, Moroccan specialty of steamed grain, broth, meats,
   vegetables and other ingredients

couscous royal, *couscous* w/meat

cousinat, bean, bell pepper, artichoke, tomato, green onion and
   carrot dish

couteau, knife   *Couteau - coo·toe.*

couvert, cover charge/place setting

couvert, vin et service compris, the price includes wine, tip and cover charge

crabe, crab

crabe verte, shore crab

crapaudine, grilled game or poultry dish

craquelins, cookies

Crécy, à la, served w/carrots

crème, cream/creamy soup/creamy dessert. Can also refer to sweet liqueur as in *crème de menthe. À la crème* means served w/a cream sauce

crème à la vanille, vanilla custard

crème allégée, light cream

crème anglaise, custard

crème brûlée, custard dessert topped w/caramelized sugar

crème caramel, vanilla custard w/caramel sauce

crème catalane, caramel-covered trifle w/cinnamon and anise

crème champignons, cream of mushroom soup

crème chantilly, vanilla-flavored and sweetened whipped cream

crème d'asperges, cream of asparagus soup

crème de cacao, cocoa-flavored liqueur

crème de cassis, black currant liqueur

crème de marrons, chestnut purée

crème de menthe, mint-flavored liqueur

crème de poireaux, cream of leek soup

crème de poulet, cream of chicken soup

crème de volaille, cream of chicken soup

We like anything with crème attached.

crème épaisse, heavy cream

crème fouettée, whipped cream

crème fraîche, thick, heavy cream

crème frit, fried cream custard dessert from Burgundy

crème glacée, ice cream

crème pâtissière, custard filling in cakes and pastry

crème plombières, custard filled w/fresh fruit

crème renversée, custard dessert in a mold

crèmerie, store selling dairy products

cremets, cream made in molds w/fruit

crêpe, crepe (thin pancake). Popular in Brittany

crêpe froment, buckwheat crepe w/sweet filling

crêpe Suzette, crepe w/orange sauce, flamed w/orange liqueur

crépine, caul fat (fat covering the intestines) used to wrap *pâtés* and *terrines*

crépinette, small sausage patty wrapped in caul fat

cresson, watercress

cressonade, watercress sauce

cressonière, watercress soup

crête de coq, cock's comb *YES, they eat this.*
  (the fleshy crest on the head of fowl)

creuse, a type of oyster

crevette, shrimp

crevette grise, gray, small shrimp

crevette rose, red shrimp w/firm flesh

cristallisés, crystallized

crist-marine, algae

croissant, crescent-shaped flaky breakfast
  roll made of flour, eggs and butter

croquant, crispy

croquants, crispy honey or almond cookies

croque madame, toasted ham and
  cheese sandwich topped w/an egg

Croquembouche. Typically served at weddings.

croquembouche, cream-puff tree

croque monsieur, toasted ham
  and cheese sandwich

croquette, ground meat, fish or vegetables
  coated in bread crumbs and deep fried

crosse, shank

crottin/croutin de chavignol, a firm
  goat cheese

croustade, pie filled w/meat, seafood and/or vegetables

croustillant, crisp/spicy *← Yes, please.*

croûte, crust

croûte au fromage, melted cheese served on a slice of toast

croûte de sel, en, in a salt crust

croûte, en, in a pastry crust

croûte forestière, mushrooms on toast

croûtes, croutons

croûton, small toasted piece of bread, usually served in a salad

cru, raw. On a wine list, this means vintage

cru classé, high-quality wine

crudités, raw vegetables

crustacé, shellfish (crustaceans) *cuiller ~*

cuiller, spoon *Qui-air*

cuillère, à la, a dish eaten w/a spoon

cuisine, there are four categories of French cuisine:

    Cuisine campagnarde (also known as
        cuisine des provinces):
        Traditional regional dishes prepared
        with fresh ingredients.

    Cuisine bourgeoise: French home cooking.

    Haute cuisine: An elaborate meal with many
        courses featuring
        rich and fresh ingredients.

    Nouvelle cuisine: Light sauces and small portions that
        emphasize the colors and textures of the ingredients.

cuisse, leg and thigh (denotes dark meat)

cuisse de poulet, chicken drumstick w/thigh

cuisses de grenouilles, frogs' legs

cuissot, haunch of game or veal

cuit, cooked

cuit à la vapeur, steamed

cuit au four, baked

cul, haunch

cul de veau, veal pot roast

culotte, rump

cumin, cumin

curaçao, orange-flavored liqueur

curcuma, the spice turmeric (used in curry powder)

cure-dent, (served w/a) toothpick

currie/curry, curry

cuvée, blend of wines or champagne/house wine

Cynar, aperitif w/an artichoke base

darne, thick fillet of fish (often salmon)

dartois, pastry w/jam

datte, date

daube, stew

daube à la niçoise, beef or lamb stew w/red wine,
    tomatoes and onions

daube de boeuf, beef stew

daube provençal, gravy w/capers, garlic and anchovies

dauphinois, a mild cheese

daurade, white fish (usually served grilled) found in the South
    of France (sea bream)

déca, decaf

décaféiné, decaffeinated

Cuisse ~ Kweece is dark meat

déca ~ day-cah

décortiqué, shelled/peeled

déglacée, warmed up

dégustation, sampling/tasting

déjeuner, lunch

délice, a delight/a treat

délimité de qualité supérieure, on a wine bottle, this means a superior-quality wine

demi, half/small beer

demi-bouteille, half bottle

demi-deuil, usually means served w/truffles

demidoff, w/vegetables

demi-bouteille ~ deh-mee. boo-tay

demi-glace, beef-stock sauce

demi-sel, soft, salty cream cheese/salted butter

demi-sec, medium dry

demoiselle de Cherbourg, small lobster

denté, dentex (fish)

désossé, boned

dessert, dessert

diable, hot, spicy sauce (often, a strong mustard sauce)/devilled.) This is also the term for an unglazed, porous pot used to cook vegetables

diabolo, a drink usually mixed w/lemonade

diane, a brown sauce w/vinegar and peppercorns

dieppoise, shrimp and mussels served in a white wine sauce

digestif, after-dinner drink

dijonnaise, served w/mustard

dinde, turkey

dindon, turkey

dindonneau, young turkey

*dinde ~ dand
dindon~ dan-dong
dindonea~ dandon-oh*

dîner, dinner

diplomate, custard dessert w/spongecake, crystallized fruit and topped w/liqueur

discrétion, when you see this on a menu, it means that you can drink as much wine as you want (for a fixed price)

divine, *hollandaise* sauce w/sherry

dodine de canard, stuffed-duck dish

domaine, on a wine label this notes a high-quality wine

dorade, sea bream

doré(e), golden
dos, back
dos et ventre, both sides (means "back and front")
douce, sweet
doucette, salad green (a cousin of *mâche*)
douceurs, desserts
doux, mild, sweet
douzaine, dozen
dragées, candied almonds
Dubonnet, wine and brandy-based aperitif w/herbs
duchesse, potatoes mixed w/egg and forced through a pastry tube
dugléré, a white sauce w/tomatoes, shallots and white wine
duxelles, finely chopped sautéed mushrooms
eau, water
eau au syphon, w/seltzer water
eau avec gaz, carbonated water
eau de source, spring water
eau-de-vie, brandy made from
    distilled fruit juice. Sold in
    elaborate tall and thin bottles in Alsace. The term means
    "water of life." This can also refer to any spirit

Don't worry you can drink the water in France.

eau du robinet, tap water
eau glacée, iced water
eau minérale, mineral water
eau minérale gazeuse, carbonated mineral water
eau nature, tap water
eau plate, still (not sparkling) water
eau sans gaz, water w/out carbonation
écailler, oyster opener/fish scaler
échalote, shallot
échine, spareribs
éclair, pastry filled w/vanilla custard and topped
    w/chocolate icing
écrevisse, crayfish
écrevisse à la nage, crayfish
    in a white wine sauce
édam français, nutty-flavored,
    orange-colored cheese
    originally from the Netherlands

Ecrevisse.

édulcorant, artificial sweetener
effilée, thinly sliced

effiloché, thinly sliced
églefin, haddock
emballé, wrapped
embeurré, buttered/buttery
embeurrée de chou, buttered cabbage
émincé, slices of cooked meat in gravy/anything thinly sliced
émincé de veau, sauteed veal slices w/creme sauce
emmental, Swiss cheese
emporter, à, take-out foods
émulsionné, liquified

Sounds good.
Never had it.

enchaud de porc à la périgourdine, pork loin stuffed
    w/truffles. A specialty in Southwest France
encornet, small squid
endive, endive/chicory
enrubanne, layered dish
    (looks like ribbons)
entier, whole
entrecôte, rib-eye steak
entrecôte Bercy, steak w/wine sauce

Endive.

entrecôte maître d'hôtel, rib-eye steak served w/herb butter
entrecôte marchand de vin, rib-eye steak served in
    red wine sauce
Entre-Deux-Mers, a region of Bordeaux
    that produces white wine
entrée, first course/appetizer
entremets, dessert
épaule, shoulder
épeautre, a variety of wheat
éperlan, smelt
épice, spice
épicé, peppered/spicy
épicerie, small grocery store
épi de maïs, miniature corn
    on the cob (often pickled)
épinard, spinach
épinards en branches, leaf spinach
époisse, a cow's-milk cheese from Burgundy
érable, maple
escabèche, raw fish marinated in lime juice and herbs. In
    Provence, this can refer to a cold marinated sardine dish
escalope, scallop/cutlet

ÉPICERIE

*Be sure to visit
a grocery
store ~ small
or large,
they're worth
the trip.*

escalope de veau, veal scallop

escalope panée, breaded veal scallop

escalope viennoise, breaded veal
cutlet (weiner schnitzel)

escargot, snail

escargot de mer, sea snail

escargot petit-gris, small snail

escarole, a type of *endive*

Escargot.

espadon, swordfish

essence, essence

estocaficada, cod stew

estofat de boeuf, beef stew

estouffade, beef stew. Can also refer to a steamed dish

estouffados, almond butter cookies found in Provence

estragon, tarragon

esturgeon, sturgeon

et, and

Estragon.

étrille, small crab

étouffée, stewed

étuvé/étuvée, steamed

éventail, en, cut into a fan shape

express, espresso

extra-sec, very dry (champagne)

façon, in the manner of

faisan, pheasant

faisane

faisan normand, pheasant w/apples and *calvados*

faisselle, fresh cow's-milk cheese

fait à la maison, homemade

falette, stuffed breast of veal

far, prune tart

farandole, dessert and/or cheese cart

farce, spiced ground meat (usually pork) used for stuffing

farci, stuffed, as in ***chou farci*** (stuffed cabbage)
and ***tomates farcies*** (stuffed tomatoes).
In Nice, this is a dish of
stuffed vegetables

Love these

farigoule, the name in Provence for wild thyme

farine, flour

farine de blé, wheat flour

farine de maïs, corn flour

faux-filet, flank steak/sirloin steak

fécule, starch. *Fécule de pommes de terre* is potato flour used to thicken sauces and soups

fécule de maïs, cornstarch

fendant, "melting." Refers to extremely tender meat or chocolate

fenouil, fennel

féra, dace (lake salmon)

ferme, farm/farm fresh

fermier, poultry raised on a farm

feu de bois, cooked on a wood fire

Feu de bois on a sign outside a restaurant indicates that they cook with wood.

feuille, leaf

feuille de chêne, oak-leaf lettuce

feuille de laurel, bay leaf

feuille de vigne, vine leaf

feuilles farcies, grape leaves stuffed w/rice and herbs

feuilletage, puff pastry

feuilletée, puff pastry

fève, broad bean

ficelle means string.

fiadone, cheesecake found in Corsica

ficelle, small baguette. *Ficellé* means tied w/a string

figatelli, Corsican liver sausage

figue, fig

figue de barbarie, prickly pear

figues.

filet, fillet

filet à la mistral, filet of sole w/tomatoes and mushrooms

filet de boeuf, beef fillet

filet de boeuf à la Poitou, beef fillet w/chicken liver *pâté*

filet de boeuf Bordelaise, beef fillet in a red wine sauce

filet de sole, fillet of sole

filet de sole meunière, fillet of sole fried in butter

filet doria, fillet of sole w/cucumbers

filet mignon, small round beef tenderloin fillet

filet Saint-Germain, fillet of sole w/potatoes

financière, cream and Madeira wine sauce. This can also refer to a dish w/veal or chicken dumplings

fine, a fine brandy

fines de claire, oysters

fines herbes, mixture of herbs (such as parsley, chives, tarragon and thyme)

flageolets, small kidney-shaped beans

flagnarde/flaugnarde, fruit-filled cake

flamande, à la, "Flemish style" w/potatoes, stuffed cabbage leaves, vegetables, sausage and bacon

flambé(e), flaming

flamiche, savory tart (similar to a quiche)

flan, tart or crustless pie. Can also refer to the caramel custard dessert of the same name found in Spain

flanchet, flank

flet, flounder

flétan, halibut

fleur, flower. *Fleurs* are crystallized flowers used on desserts

fleurette, small flower

Fleurie, a red wine from Beaujolais

fleurons, crescent-shaped puff pastries

fleurs de courgettes farcies, zucchini flowers stuffed w/cheese

flocon, flake

flocons d'avoine, oat flakes

florentine, w/spinach

foie, liver

foie de veau, calf's liver

foie de veau grand-mère, sautéed calf's liver w/bacon, onion and potato garnish

foie de volaille, chicken liver

foie gras, fattened goose liver

foie gras de canard, fattened duck liver

foie gras d'oie, fattened goose liver

foie gras en brioche, fattened goose liver that is marinated and cooked and baked a second time in a pastry shell

foies blonds de volaille, chicken livers

foin, cooked in hay

fond, bottom ⟵ *I'd rather not.*

fondant, cake icing

fondant au chocolat, similar to a brownie (but better!)

fond d'artichaut, artichoke heart

fondu/fondue (au fromage), melted cheese in a pot. Dip your bread or meat in!

fondu aux raisins, the crust of this smooth and creamy cheese is made of grape pulp. Also known as *tomme au marc*

fondue bourguignonne, small pieces of meat dipped into oil and eaten w/sauces

fondue chinoise, thin slices of beef dipped in bouillon and eaten w/sauces

fondue savoyarde, pot of melted cheese for dipping

forestière, ("forester's style") usually means w/sautéed mushrooms

forêt noire, Black Forest cake

forme d'Ambert, a blue cheese

formule, une, a set-price menu

fort, strong (as in strong or sharp cheese)

fougasse, decorated bread loaf w/olive oil flavoring and sometimes w/bacon, onion or tomato stuffing

fougassette, a slice of *brioche* bread flavored w/orange and saffron

four, au, baked

fourchette, fork

fournée, baked

fournitures, fresh herbs and salad greens

fourré, filled/stuffed

fraîche, fresh

frais, fresh

fraise, strawberry

Fraîche - fraysh
Frais - fray
Fraise - frez

fraise des bois, wild strawberry

framboise, raspberry/raspberry liqueur

frangipane, almond custard filling

frappé, drink blended w/ice

frémis, oysters (served almost raw)

friand, meat-filled pastry

friandises, *petits fours*

fricadelles, fried meat patties

fricadelles à la bière, meatballs in beer. A specialty in Belgium

fricandeau, braised veal dish

fricassée, a stew of meat, poultry or fish finished w/cream

fricassée liégeoise, fried eggs, bacon and sausage. A specialty in Belgium

frigolet, name in Provence for wild thyme

frisée, curly endive

frit, fried

fritelli, chestnut-flour doughnuts from Corsica

frites, french fries (often eaten w/mayonnaise) *← yes!*

fritons, minced spread made of organ meats *← No.!*

fritot, batter fried or fritter

friture, frying

friture de mer/friture de poisson, fried small fish

froid, cold

Froid ~ Fwa

fromage, cheese. It is said that
there are over 400 different French cheeses

fromage à pâte dure, hard cheese

fromage à pâte molle, soft cheese

fromage au marc, a sharp, tangy cheese

I don't think so.

fromage blanc, cream cheese (but runny)

fromage de brebis, sheep's-milk cheese

fromage de chèvre, goat's-milk cheese

fromage de tête, headcheese (sausage made from the meat of a
calf's or pig's head cooked in a gelatinous meat
broth and then served cold)

fromage fermier, cheese made where the milk is produced

fromage fort, extremely soft cheese from Provence mixed
w/herbs, salt, pepper and *marc*

fromage maigre, low-fat cheese

fromagerie, cheese shop

Fruit ~ fru-ee

fruit, fruit

fruit confit, candied fruit

fruit de la passion, passion fruit

fruits de mer, seafood

fumé, smoked

fumet, fish stock

galantine, cold gelatinized meat dish

galette, buckwheat pancake. *Galettes de blé de sarrasin* are
crêpes made w/dark flour and filled w/cheese, ham,
an egg, mushrooms or any number of things.
Galettes de blé de froment are dessert crêpes made with
light flour. *Galette* can also refer to a flaky pastry "cake"
w/an almond paste filling. This is the traditional cake served
on Three Kings' Day. A bean (now a little porcelain statue is
used) is put in the cake and the person who gets the piece
containing the bean is king or queen for the day and wears a
a gold crown

galette bretonne, butter and rum cake

galette de pommes, apple tart

galette de sarrasin, buckwheat pancake w/savoury filling
popular in Brittany

galopin, bread pancake

Gamay de Touraine, red wine made w/the Gamay grape

gambas, large prawns

gambas à la planxa, grilled shrimp served on a plank of wood

ganses, fried cakes topped w/sugar

garbure, cabbage soup. In Southern France, this is usually cabbage soup w/ham

garni(e), w/vegetables/garnished

garniture, vegetables/garnished

gâteau, cake

gâteau au chocolat, chocolate cake

gâteau au fromage, cheese tart

gâteau de Savoie, spongecake

gâteau de riz, rice pudding

gateau ~ gat-oh

gaufre, waffle. A specialty in Belgium

gaufrette, sweet wafer

gayettes, small sausage patties

gazeuse, carbonated.

Non-gazeuse means not carbonated

gelé, frozen

gelée, jellied/in aspic

gélinotte, prairie chicken

genièvre, juniper berry

génoise, spongecake

Gelée. Hmmm. not something we eat with gusto.

germiny, sorrel and cream soup/w/sorrel

gésier, gizzard

Gewürztraminer, dry white wine from Alsace

gibelotte de lapin, rabbit stew

gibier, game

gigot, leg

gigot d'agneau, leg of lamb

gigot de mer, oven-roasted monkfish dish

gigot de mouton pré-salé, leg of lamb dish made w/lambs that graze in salt meadows in Northwest France

gigot farci, stuffed leg of lamb

gigue, the haunch of game meat

gimblettes, ring cookies

gin, gin

gingembre, ginger

gin tonique, gin and tonic

girofle, clove

girolle, chanterelle mushroom

glaçage, frosting

glace, ice/ice cream

glacé, iced/glazed

glace à la napolitaine, layers of different-flavored ice cream

glace au fondant, shiny cake icing

glace crémeuse, ice cream

glace de viande, concentrated meat stock (meat glaze)

glace de poisson, concentrated fish stock

glaçons, ice

globe, round (cut of meat)

gnocchi, gnocchi (potato dumplings). Found frequently on menus in Nice and near the Italian border

gnocchi aux blettes, gnocchi w/Swiss chard incorporated into the dough

gougère, cheese-flavored pastry ⟵ *Oui, s'il vous plaît.*

goujon, gudgeon (related to carp)

goujonnettes, small slices of fish

gourmandises, sweets/candies

gousse, clove

gousse d'ail, clove of garlic

goûter, snack/to taste

graine, grain/seed

graine de maïs, corn meal

graine de moutarde, mustard seed

graines de paradis, similar to the spice cardamom and found in the former French African colonies

graisse, fat

graisserons, fried pieces of goose or duck skin *graisserons. These are like cracklings and used as garnish.*

grand, large

grand crème, a large milky coffee

grand cru, high-quality wine

Grand Marnier, orange liqueur

grand-mère, means "grandmother." A garnish usually of mushrooms, potatoes and bacon

grand veneur, brown sauce w/red currants (usually served w/game)

grand vin, high-quality wine

granité, slushy iced drink

gras, fat/fatty

gras-double, tripe simmered in wine and onions

gratin, au, topped w/grated cheese, breadcrumbs and butter and then baked

gratin dauphinois, potato au gratin dish w/eggs, cheese and cream

gratin de fruits de mer, shellfish in a cream sauce

gratin de queues d'écrevisses, freshwater crayfish served *au gratin*

gratin de capucins, *gratin* of stuffed artichoke hearts

gratin savoyard, baked sliced-potato casserole

gratiné, prepared w/breadcrumbs

gratinée, topped w/cheese/onion soup

grattons, fried pieces of pork, goose or duck skin

gratuit, free

Graves, wine region of Bordeaux

grecque, cold vegetable mixture (*légumes à la grecque*). *À la grecque* refers to dishes stewed in oil (in the Greek style)

grelot, small white onion

grenade, pomegranate

grenadin, small veal scallop

grenoblois, caramel-walnut cake

grenouille, frog

gribiche, mayonnaise w/gherkins and capers. *Sauce gribiche* can refer to a vinaigrette and egg sauce

grillade, grilled meat/mixed grill

grillé, grilled

griotte, a type of cherry (usually in white alcohol)

grive, thrush (a bird)

grondin, spiked-headed ocean fish (gurnet)

gros bout de poitrine, brisket

groseille, currant

groseille à maquereau, gooseberry/currant

groseille rouge, red currant

gros sel, coarse salt

Gruyère

grumes, heavy coating or skin

gruyère, Swiss cheese

guimauve, marshmallow

haché, hashed

hachis, hash

hachis parmentier, shepherd's pie (ground meat and mashed potatoes topped w/a white sauce and served in a casserole)

hareng, herring

harengs fumés à la Créole, spicy smoked herring dish flamed
in rum (found in the French West Indies)
haricot, bean
haricot de mer, tiny clam
haricot de mouton, mutton, bean
and potato stew
haricot de soisson, navy bean/kidney bean
haricot rouge, red kidney bean
haricots en salade, bean salad
haricots verts, green beans (french beans)
Henri IV, artichoke hearts and *béarnaise* sauce
herbes, herbs
herbes de Provence, mixture of herbs that includes fennel,
lavender, marjoram, bay leaf, sage, rosemary and thyme
hérisson de mer, sea urchin
hochepot, oxtail stew
hollandaise, sauce of melted butter, egg yolks and lemon juice
homard, lobster
homard à l'américaine, flaming lobster dish w/white wine,
herbs, tomatoes and garlic
homard à l'armoricaine, lobster in a tomato sauce
homard cardinal, flaming lobster dish w/mushrooms and truffles
homard froid à la parisienne, cold lobster garnished w/diced
vegetables in a mayonnaise sauce
homard Newburg, lobster cooked in a sauce made of butter,
cream, wine (or brandy) and egg yolks
homard Thermidor, flaming lobster dish w/white wine, herbs,
spices and mustard
hongroise, served w/paprika and cream (means "Hungarian")
hors-d'oeuvre, appetizer
huile, oil
huile d'arachide, peanut oil
huile de carthame, safflower oil
huile de noix, walnut oil
huile de soya, soybean oil
huile de tournesol, sunflower oil
huile d'olive (vierge), olive oil (virgin)
huître, oyster
huître belon, pink oyster
huître portugaise, Portuguese lobster (small and fat)
hure de porc, pig's head

Haricots.

We like the name.

*Hors d'oeuvre.
means
without
work.*

hure de saumon, salmon pâté
hysope, the bitter herb hysop
île flottante, meringues floating
    in a cream sauce
impératrice, rice-pudding dessert
importée, imported
indienne, w/curry (in the style of India)
infusion, herbal tea
jalousies, apricot pastry
jambe, leg
jambon, ham
jambon à l'os, baked ham
jambon blanc, boned, cooked ham
jambon cuit, cooked ham
jambon cuit d'Ardennes, smoked ham found in Belgium
jambon de Bayonne, raw, salty ham
jambon de canard, cured, salted or smoked duck or
    goose breast
jambon de montagne, local cured ham
jambon de Paris, lightly salted ham
jambon de Parme, Parma ham (prosciutto)
jambon de pays, local "country" cured ham
jambon de York, smoked ham (English style)
jambon d'oie, cured, salted or smoked duck or goose breast
jambon cru, cured ham
jambonneau, pork knuckle
jambon persillé, parsleyed ham
jardinière, w/diced vegetables
jarret, shank/knuckle
jarret de veau, veal shank
    (usually a stew)
jerez, sherry (Spanish for sherry)
Jésus de Morteau, smoked pork sausage
jeune, young/green (as in unripe)
joue, cheek
jour, du, of the day
jud mat gardebóneh, smoked pork and
    bean dish found in Luxembourg
julienne, vegetables cut into fine strips.
    There is also a fish w/this name
jumeau, pot roast

Handwritten note (top right): île Flottante... don't see the appeal of this but it's very popular.

Handwritten note (middle right): à l'os means bone-in.

Handwritten note (lower, with arrow): Never warmed up to this

Jura, one of France's wine-growing regions
jus, juice/gravy
jus de tomate, tomato juice
jus d'orange, orange juice
kaki, persimmon
kalouga, chocolate-pudding cake
ketchup, ketchup
kig-ha-farz, buckwheat pudding
    w/vegetables and meat
kir, apéritif made w/*crème de cassis* and wine
kir royal, apéritif made w/champagne and *crème de cassis*
kirsch, cherry-flavored liqueur
kougelhopf/kouglof/kugelhopf, Alsatian cake w/raisins
    and almonds
kouigh amann, buttered pastry
l', la, le, the (singular). *Les* is the (plural)
lait, milk
laitance, fish roe
lait de beurre, buttermilk
lait écrémé, skim milk
lait entier, whole milk
laitue, lettuce
lambi, conch found in the French West Indies
lamelle, very thin slice
lamproie, lamprey
langouste, crayfish
langouste à la sètoise, lobster (crawfish) w/garlic, tomatoes and
    cognac
langoustine, prawn
langue, tongue
langue de chat, biscuit and ice-cream dessert
Languedoc, one of France's wine-growing regions
languedocienne, usually means eggplant,
    tomato and mushroom garnish
lapereau, young rabbit
lapin, rabbit
lapin à l'artésienne, rabbit stew
lapin à la Lorraine, rabbit in a
    mushroom and cream sauce
lapin aux pruneaux, rabbit w/prunes.
    A popular dish in Northern France

Handwritten notes:

Jus d'orange is usually served with water and sugar.

Lamproie — yikes.

Langue de chat means cat's tongue.

Lapin Sworn enemy of all gardeners.

lapin chasseur, rabbit in a white wine and herb sauce
lapin de garenne, wild rabbit
lapin en paquets, rabbit pieces in a packet
    of bacon. A specialty in Provence
lard, bacon
lardon, diced bacon
laurier, bay leaf

Laurier.

lavande, lavender. Lavender blossoms are added to dishes in
    Provence such as *sorbet de lavande* (lavender sorbet)
lèche, thin slice (usually of meat or bread)
léger, light
légère, light (as in light beer)
légumes, vegetables
lentilles, lentils
levraut, young rabbit
levure, yeast
libre service, self-service
lieu, small saltwater fish
lièvre, rabbit (hare)
lièvre en cabessal, stuffed hare dish
limande, dab (flounder)
limande sole, lemon sole
limonade, lemonade-flavored soft drink

Limonade is a carbonated soft drink.

liqueur, liqueur
lisette, small mackerel
lit, bed (as in a bed of lettuce)
litre, liter. Wine is often served in a liter carafe, *demi-litre*
    (half-liter) or *un quart* (quarter-liter)
livarot, round, sharp, tangy cheese
Loire, this valley is one of France's wine regions along the
    Loire River
longe, loin. *Longe de veau* is loin of veal
longeole, pork sausage stuffed w/cabbage, leeks and spinach.
    A specialty in French-speaking Switzerland
lonzu, shoulder (in Corsica)
lorraine, usually braised in red wine w/cabbage
lotte, monkfish
loubine, fish similar to sea bass
lou cachat, crushed cheese
lou magret, breast of fattened goose or duck
lou mäis, corn-meal cake found in Provence

Lou means "the" in Provençal.

loup/loup de mer, sea bass. *Loup au fenouille* is sea bass grilled over fennel stalks

lou pevre, goat's-milk cheese w/coarsely ground pepper

lou piech, stuffed veal dish found around Nice

louvine, fish similar to sea bass

Lucullus, dish that contains extremely rich and/or rare ingredients. Named after a Roman general who hosted great feasts

lyonnaise, sautéed w/mushrooms and/or onions/sauce of onions, butter and white wine ("Lyon style")

macaron, macaroon. Not the sticky coconut version found at home, but two almond-meringue cookies, flavored with vanilla, chocolate, coffee, pistachio or other flavors, stuck together with butter cream

macaroni au gratin, macaroni and cheese

macédoine, mixed fruit or mixed vegetables

macédoine de légumes, mixed vegetables

macérer, to pickle or soak

mâche, a type of lettuce

macis, the outer covering of a nutmeg/mace

Mâcon, wine from Burgundy

mache.

mâconnaise, usually refers to a goat's milk cheese

macreuse, pot roast

madeleine, butter cake

madère, w/Madeira wine

magret, breast of fattened goose or duck

maigre, lean. *Filet de maigre* usually refers to white fish

maïs, corn

maison, house

maître d'hôtel, head waiter/sautéed in butter w/lemon juice and parsley

maltaise, orange-flavored *hollandaise* sauce

mandarine, tangerine

mange-tout, snow pea/type of apple

mangue, mango

manière, de, in the style of

mange-tout means eat all

maquereau, mackerel

maraîchère, usually means w/various greens (market style)

marbré, marbled

marc, a strong liqueur made from distilling the residue of grapes (similar to Italian *grappa*). *Marc de Bandol* is a popular *marc* found in Provence

marcassin, young wild boar
marchand de vin, red wine and shallot sauce/wine merchant
marché, market
marée, a term used to denote fresh seafood (literally "the tide")
Marengo, à la, w/eggs
marennes, flat-shelled oysters
margarine, margarine (almost never served in Paris)
Margaux, a red wine from Bordeaux
mariné, marinated
marinière, "sailor's style" usually means w/seafood (most
    often mussels) simmered in herbs and white wine
marjolaine, marjoram. This can also refer to a layered
    chocolate and nut cake
marmelade, marmalade
marmite, food cooked in a small casserole *Marquise...*
marquise, mousse cake *don't miss*
maroilles, strong, hard cheese *having this.*
marron, chestnut
marrons au sirop, chestnuts in vanilla-flavored syrup
marrons chauds, roasted chestnuts.
    Served on the streets of Paris
marrons entiers au naturel, chestnuts in water
    (used in stuffing, sauces or as a vegetable)
marrons glacés, candied chestnuts
marrons Mont Blanc, chestnut purée
    and cream on a spongecake soaked in rum
massepain, marzipan
matafan, simple cake (flour, butter, milk and eggs) made in a
    skillet
matelote, freshwater fish stew/fish stew (usually eel) w/wine
    from the French West Indies. *Matelote de veau* is veal stew
    w/red wine
mauresque, a drink of *pastis* w/almond and orange syrup
mauviette, meadow lark
mayonnaise, mayonnaise
médaillon, small, round cut of meat
Médoc, red wine from Bordeaux
mélange, mixture/blend
mélasses, molasses
méli-mélo, assorted seafood
méli-mélo de légumes, mixed vegetables

melon, cantaloupe

melon à l'italienne, melon w/*prosciutto*

melon d'eau, watermelon. The French call it ***pastèque***

melon de Cavaillon, similar to a canteloupe

ménagère, a basic preparation usually w/carrots, potatoes and/or onions (means "in the style of a housewife")

mendiants, dessert made of dry figs, raisins, almonds and nuts

menthe, mint

menthe poivrée, peppermint

menu, menu (often a fixed-price meal)

menu dégustation, set-price gourmet menu of specialties of the chef

Menu dequstation is usually better Quality.

menu du jour, menu of the day

menu fixe, fixed-price menu

menu gastronomique, gourmet menu

menu pour enfant, children's menu

mer, sea

merda, *gnocchi* made w/Swiss chard

merenda, morning snack

merguez, spicy sausage (usually lamb)

meringues, baked shells of sweetened, beaten egg whites

merlan, whiting

merle, blackbird

Merle.

Merlot, dry, medium- to full-bodied red wine

merlu, a type of hake

merluche, dried cod

mérou, grouper

merveille, sugar doughnut

mesclun, lettuce salad of mixed greens *No thanks.*

messine, an herb and cream sauce

méthode champenoise, sparkling wine (natural method)

mets, dish/preparation

mets selon la saison, seasonal preparation

meunière, w/parsley butter/seasoned fish floured and fried in butter, lemon and parsley. The word means "miller's wife" which refers to the flour that is used to prepare this dish

meurette, w/red wine sauce

Meursault, wine from Burgundy

miel, honey

miel Lavan

miettes, flakes/crumbs

mignardises, *petits fours* (small fancy cookies or cakes)
mignon, tenderloin cut
mignonette, small piece of fillet/coarsely ground white pepper
mijoté, simmered
milieu de poitrine, brisket
millas, corn-meal mush
mille-feuille, light pastry w/cream filling (napoleon)
millésime, vintage
mimolette, a mild cheese
mimosa, w/chopped egg yolks
mirabeau, w/anchovies and olives
mirabelle, yellow plum/plum brandy
mireilie, à la, there are many versions
    of this cold marinade

Mille feuille means a thousand leaves.

mirepoix, vegetables cut into cubes
miroir pommes, apple-Bavarian cream dessert
miroton, slices. Can also refer to a meat and onion stew or a
    brown sauce including onions
mitonnée, a souplike dish
mixte, mixed
mode, à la, in the style of
moelle, bone/marrow
moelleux, full-bodied. This can also mean tender
moka, coffee
mollusques, shellfish
momie, thimble-sized *pastis*
montagne, de, from the mountains
Mont Blanc, chestnut meringue topped w/a "mountain" of
    whipped cream (named after the mountain peak)
montmorency, w/cherries
morceau, piece
morille, morel mushroom (a rare,
    wild mushroom w/a smoky flavor)

morceau~ mor-So

mornay, white sauce w/cheese
mortadelle, bologna sausage
    w/pistachios and pickles
morue, salt cod
morue en rayte, cod in red wine sauce
moscovite, a dessert made in a mold w/any number of
    ingredients/a way of preparing duck
mouclade, creamy mussel soup

moule, mussel

moule de bouchot, small cultivated mussel

moule d'Espagne, large sharp-shelled mussel (frequently served raw)

moule de Parques, Dutch cultivated mussel

moules à la crème, mussels in white wine w/cream

moules à la poulette, mussels in a rich white wine sauce

moules marinières, mussels simmered in white wine w/shallots

mourtayrol, chicken dish flavored w/saffron

moussaka, a Greek dish frequently found on menus in Paris. It is an eggplant, lamb and tomato casserole

mousse, a light and airy dish of whipped cream or beaten egg whites/chopped meat or fish w/eggs and cream

mousse au chocolat, chocolate mousse

mousse de foie gras, *foie gras* must have, under French law, fattened liver w/up to 20% other foods. *Mousse de foie gras* contains up to 45% other foods such as eggs, pork liver and/or truffles

mousseline, w/whipped cream/*hollandaise* sauce w/cream

mousseron, small wild mushroom

mousseux, sparkling

moutarde, mustard

mouton, mutton

muge, mullet (in Provence)

mulet, mullet

munster, full-bodied cheese, often flavored w/caraway, cumin or anise)

mûre, blackberry

muscade, nutmeg

Muscadet, a dry, white wine

muscat, dessert wine

museau, muzzle

museau de veau, calf's muzzle

myrtille, blueberry

mystère, cooked meringue dessert w/ice cream

nage, "swimming;" served in an aromatic poaching liquid

nantua, crayfish or shrimp sauce

napolitaine, vanilla, strawberry and chocolate ice cream

nappe, tablecloth

nappé, covered in a sauce

nature, plain

MUzzle... sounds grim.

myrtille ~ mir - tee.

naturel, plain. *Au naturel* means plainly cooked
navarin, mutton stew w/turnips
navet, turnip
nefle, small orange-colored fruit
nègre, flourless chocolate cake
neige, w/beaten egg whites (means "snow")
neufchâtel, rich, creamy cheese (a lower-fat cheese)
Newburg, lobster cooked in a sauce made of butter, cream,
 wine (or brandy) and egg yolks. Newburg is an alteration
 of Wenburg, the name of the patron for whom the
 sauce was named
niçoise, usually means w/tomatoes, anchovies, vinegar and
 black olives. Named after the city of Nice
nid d'abeilles, honey cake
nivernaise , à la, a dish w/carrots and onions
Noilly Prat, French vermouth
noir, black
noisette, hazelnut/round piece of meat
noix, nut/walnut. This can also refer to nuggets
noix d'acajou, cashew
noix de coco, coconut
noix de muscade, nutmeg
noix de pecan, pecan
noix de veau, top side of the leg of veal
non, not or no
nonats, tiny Mediterranean fish served deep fried
normande, usually means cooked w/fish, cream and mushrooms
 ("Normandy style"). This can also refer to a dish in a
 cream sauce often w/*calvados*
nougats, roasted almonds, egg whites, nuts and honey dessert
nouilles, noodles
nouilles fraîches maison, homemade fresh pasta
nouveau, new
nouveauté, new offering
nouvelle, new
noyau, pit (as in an olive pit)
Nuits-Saint-Georges, high-quality red wine from Burgundy
oeuf, egg. *Blancs d'oeufs* are egg whites
 and *jaunes d'oeufs* are egg yolks
oeuf à la coque, soft-boiled egg
oeuf à l'américaine, fried egg

Navarin... I'll pass.

abeille~ bee

Noisette can also mean a small cup of café crème.

Oeuf à la coque — egg in the shell.

95

oeuf à la russe, hard-boiled egg served cold w/diced vegetables in mayonnaise

oeuf à l'Huguenote, poached egg w/meat sauce

oeuf au plat, fried egg

oeuf brouillé, scrambled egg

oeuf chemise, poached egg

oeuf Côte d'Azur, poached egg in an artichoke bottom

oeuf dur, hard-boiled egg

oeuf dur soubise, hard-boiled egg w/onion and cream sauce

oeuf en gelée, poached egg served in gelatin

oeuf en meurette, poached egg in a red wine sauce

oeuf farci, stuffed egg

oeuf frit, fried egg

oeuf mayonnaise, eggs and mayonnaise

oeuf mollet, soft-boiled egg

oeuf poché, poached egg

oeuf poché à la Chartres, poached egg w/tarragon

oeuf Rossini, egg w/truffles and Madeira wine. This can also be a poached egg w/*pâté*

oeufs à la diable, devilled eggs

oeufs à la neige, whipped, sweetened egg whites served in a vanilla custard sauce (means "eggs in the snow")

oeufs au lait, egg custard

oeuf sauté à la poêle, fried egg

oeufs au vin, eggs poached in red wine

oeufs d'alose, cooked fish (shad) eggs

oeufs en meurette, poached eggs w/red wine sauce from Bourgogne

oeufs fermier, eggs from poultry raised on a farm

oeufs pochés suzettes, poached eggs in baked potatoes

oeuf sur la plat, fried egg

offert, free ("offered")

oie, goose

oie à l'instar de visé, goose boiled and then fried. A Belgian specialty

oignon, onion

oignons grelots, small pickled onions

oiseau, bird

olives, olives

olives farcies, stuffed olives

olives noires, black olives

Oie.

Oiseau~
wazoe

96

olives vertes, green olives
omble-chevalier, freshwater fish of the trout family (char)
omelette, omelet
omelette au fromage, cheese omelet
omelette au jambon, ham omelet
omelette au lard, bacon omelet
omelette au naturel, plain omelet
omelette aux champignons, mushroom omelet
omelette aux fines herbs, omelet w/herbs
omelette brayaude, potato omelet
omelette César, omelet w/garlic and herbs
omelette complète, omelet w/ham and cheese
omelette fourée aux pommes dite à la Normande, apple
    upside-down cake
omelette landaise, omelet w/pine nuts
omelette nature, plain omelet
omelette norvégienne, baked Alaska
omelette parmentier, potato omelet
omelette paysanne, omelet w/bacon and potatoes
omelette quercynoise, cheese and walnut omelet
onglet, hanger steak
opéra, layered spongecake w/chocolate sauce
orange, orange
orange givrée, orange sorbet served in an orange
orange pressée, fresh, squeezed orange juice
oranges en rondelles, candied orange slices in orange jelly
oreilles, ears
oreillettes, pastry puffs
orge, barley
orgeat, almond-sugar syrup
origon, oregano
orties, nettles
ortolan, small game bird
os, bone
os à moelle, marrow bone
oseille, sorrel (an herb eaten as a leafy vegetable)
ostendaise, w/shrimp and oysters
ou, or
ouassous, large crayfish found in the French West Indies
oursin, sea urchin
pacanes, pecans (in Guadeloupe)

Olives Farcies.

Ortolans are eaten whole, everything but the beak. They're illegal to serve.

paëlla, saffron-flavored rice and various ingredients. There are many variations of this famous Spanish dish found on menus all over France

pagre commun, sea bream

paillard, thin, flattened piece of meat, poultry or fish fillet

pailles pommes, fried, shredded potatoes

paillettes, cheese straws

pain, bread

pain au chocolat, chocolate-filled pastry *Pain ~*

pain au lait, sweet bun *Pan*

pain aux noix, walnut bread

pain aux raisins, bun w/custard and white raisins

pain blanc, white bread

pain complet, whole-wheat bread

pain de campagne, chewy "country" bread

pain de mie, sliced white bread (sandwich bread)

pain d'épices, gingerbread/a dense spice cake w/honey

pain de seigle, rye bread

pain de son, bran bread

pain de sucre, sugar loaf *Bread is buttered at breakfast but not lunch or dinner.*

pain grillé, toast

pain noir, dark bread

pain ordinaire, French bread

pain perdu, French toast. Literally, "lost bread" invented because French bread has no preservatives, thus becomes hard very quickly. The milk and eggs soften the bread

pain viennois, Vienna loaf

palaia, small sardines and anchovies

palais, cookies. *Palais de dames* are fruit cookies

paleron, shoulder of beef

paletot, skin, bone and meat of a fattened goose or duck (after the liver is removed)

palets de marrons, puréed-chestnut patties

palette de porc, pork shoulder

palmiers, palm hearts (*coeurs de palmier*). This can also refer to a caramelized puff pastry

paloise, *béarnaise* sauce w/mint

palombe, pigeon

palourdes, clams

pamplemousse, grapefruit *Always liked that word.*

panaché, mixed. *Un panaché* also refers to a drink made of half beer and half lemon soda

panade, thick mixture used to bind dumplings (panada)

panais, parsnip

pan bagnat, large round sandwich filled w/olive oil, onions, olives, tomatoes, anchovies and a hard-boiled egg. A specialty on the Côte d'Azur (means "wet bread"). This is a *salade niçoise* sandwich

pané, breaded

panier, basket

panisses, chickpea-flour pancake (deep fried)

panne de porc, fat from the kidneys of a pig

pannequet, rolled, filled crêpe

papalines, orange-flavored chocolates from Avignon

papeton d'aubergines, eggplant casserole from Avignon (means "eggplant of the popes")

papillons, butterfly cookies. This can also refer to a type of oyster

papillote, en, baked in parchment paper

paquets, en, in packages or parcels

parfait, ice-cream dessert. Can also refer to goose, duck or chicken-liver mousse

parfum, flavor

Paris-Brest, ring-shaped *éclair* filled w/praline cream

parisienne, a vegetable garnish w/potatoes sautéed in butter w/a white sauce

parme, amberjack (in Provence)

parmentier, dish containing potatoes

part, portion

partager, to share

passe-pierre, seaweed

Passe-Tout-Grain, red wine from Burgundy

pasta, pasta. Originally from neighboring Italy, pasta is an important part of Provençal cuisine

Pastèque.

pastèque, watermelon

pastilles, hard, fruit- or mint-flavored candy

pastis, anise-flavored aperitif. This is a Provençal word meaning mixture. It is a summer drink. Common brands are Pastis 51, Pernod, Ricard, Granier, Prado and Henri Bardouin

pastis landais, a sweet bread dessert

patate, sweet potato
patate douce, sweet potato
pâte, pastry dough.
 This can also mean a batter or paste.
 Do not confuse this w/*pâté* or *pâtes*
pâte à choux, cream-puff pastry
pâte à foncer, shortbread crust
pâte à frire, sweet french-frying batter
pâte à pain, bread dough
pâte brisée, pie pastry
pâte d'amandes, marzipan
pâte de fruits, fruit-paste candies
pâte feuilletée, puff pastry
pâte levée, bread dough
pâte sablée, sweet pie pastry
pâte sucrée, sweet pie pastry
pâté, pâté
pâté ardennais, purée of pork in a loaf of bread
pâté de campagne, *pâté* w/a variety of meats
pâté de canard, duck *pâté*
pâté de foie de volaille, chicken-liver *pâté*
pâté de foie d'oie, *pâté* that contains at least 50% goose liver and
 up to 50% other meats
pâté de foie gras, goose-liver *pâté*. Contains at least 75% goose
 liver
pâté doré, seasoned baked pork-liver *pâté* served cold
pâté en croûte, *pâté* in a pastry crust
pâté en pot, mutton soup found in the French West Indies
pâté maison et rillettes, a slice of a loaf of ground seasoned meat
patranque, bread andbacon pancake
pâtes, pasta
pâtisserie, pastry
patranque, bread and bacon pancake
patte, foot (paw) or leg of an animal or bird
patte blanche, small crayfish
patte rouge, large crayfish
Pauillac, rich red wine from Bordeaux
paupiette, slice of veal or beef rolled around stuffing
pavé, thick slice of beef (or calf's liver)
pavé aux marrons, chestnut and chocolate cake
pavot, graines de, poppy seeds

Pâte is pastry.
Pâté is pâté.
Pâtes is pasta.

Patte blanche.

paysanne, à la, "country style" usually means a
  dish containing assorted vegetables
pays d'auge, cream and cider sauce
pays, du, from the area
peau, skin
pêche, peach
pêche melba, peaches w/ice cream and raspberry sauce
pêcheur, this term refers to fish preparations (means
  "fisherman")
pelardons, goat cheese
pelé, peeled
pelure, peelings
perce-pierre, seaweed
perche, perch
perdreau, young partridge
perdrix, partridge
périgourdine, à la, w/goose- or duck-liver purée and truffles
périgueux, a brown sauce w/chopped truffles
Pernod, anise-flavored aperitif
perroquet, a drink of *pastis* and mint
persil, parsley. *Persillé* means parslied
persillade, chopped parsley and garlic
pesto, see *pistou*
pétillant, slightly sparkling beverage
petit, small
petit beurre, tea biscuit
petit déjeuner, breakfast
petite friture, fried whitebait
petit four, small fancy cookie or cake
petit gâteau, small cake/cookie
petit-gris, small snail
petit noir, black coffee
petit pain, roll. *Petits pains au maïs* are made w/corn meal
petit pois, pea
petit pois de cérons, peas w/pork   *Petits Pois.*
petit salé, salt pork
petits farcis provençaux, stuffed vegetables of Provence
petits gâteaux, cookies
petits pois, peas
petits pois à la Normande, creamed peas
petit-suisse, creamy, unsalted cheese/cheese *beignets*

pétoncle, tiny scallop
pets de nonne, small fried pastry *Pichet*
pibale, small eel
pichet, pitcher of wine *Pee-shay*
picodon, goat's-milk cheese from Provence
picon bière, beer mixed w/a sweet liqueur
pièce, piece/each
pied, foot
pied de cochon, pig's foot
pied de mouton, wild mushroom/sheep's foot
pied de porc, pig's foot
pieps et paquets, stuffed-tripe dish
pietra, chestnut-flavored beer from Corsica
pieuvre, octopus
pigeon, pigeon
pigeonneau, young pigeon
pignatelle, small cheese fritter
pignons, pine nuts/croissant w/pine nuts
pilaf/pilau, rice cooked w/broth and onions
piment, chili pepper/pimento
piment doux, sweet pepper
piment en poudre, chili powder
piment poivre de Jamaïque, allspice *Piment doux*
pimprenelle, burnet (a green used in salads)
pince, claw
pineau, cognac and grape juice
pintade, guinea hen
pintadeau, young guinea hen
pipérade, omelet w/ham, green peppers, tomatoes and garlic
piquant, spicy hot
piquante, sauce of pickles or capers, shallots and vinegar
piqué, larded
pissala, fish purée used in *pissaladière*
pissaladière, pizza-like tart w/onions,
    black olives and purée of anchovies
    and sardines (from Provence)
pissenlit, dandelion leaves
pistache, pistachio
pistil de safran, thread of saffron
pistou, garlic, basil, nuts and olive oil sauce (known as pesto in
    Italy)/pesto soup

pithiviers, puff pastry filled w/ground almonds and sweet cream
pizza, pizza is not shared in France, is not eaten w/your
hands and will be served w/a bottle of olive oil w/hot
peppers at the bottom. The oil is to spice up your pizza.
A cheese and tomato pizza is called a *marguerite*
pizza quatres saisons, four-seasons pizza (four toppings: ham,
mushrooms, cheese and anchovy)
pizza reine, pizza topped w/ham and mushrooms
planteurs, rum and fruit punches found in the French West Indies
plaque de chocolat, chocolate bar
plat, plate/dish
plat de résistance, main course
plat du jour, plate (special) of the day
plate, flat-shelled oyster. This can also
refer to water w/out carbonation
plateau, platter
plateau de fromages, platter of cheeses. In Normandy, this is
almost always served w/*calvados*
plat froid, cold plate
plat minceur, diet plate
plat principal (plats principaux),
main course(s)
pleurote, grey mushroom
found in the Loire Valley
plie, flounder/plaice
plie franche, flounder
plombières, vanilla ice-cream dessert
w/whipped cream and candied fruit
pluviers, plovers (small birds)
poché, poached
pochouse, fish and onion stew
prepared w/wine (from Bourgogne)
poêle, à la, fried
point, à, medium done. In France,
this means still pink
pointe, tip. *Pointe d'asperge* is
an asparagus tip
poire, pear
poireau (poireaux), leek(s)
poire Belle Hélène, pear w/ice cream and chocolate sauce
poirier d'anjou, pear cake

*Plat minceur.
I hope you're
just looking this
up to see what
it is, not
ordering it!*

Plie.

*A poêle is
a frying pan.*

pois, peas
pois chiche, chick-pea
pois mange-tout, snow pea
poisson, fish
poisson à grande friture, deep-dried fish
poisson d'eau douce, freshwater fish
poisson de mer, saltwater fish
poissonnerie, fish soup/fish store
poitrine, breast
poitrine d'agneau Sainte Menehould, braised and grilled
    lamb breast
poitrine demi-sel, slab of unsmoked bacon
poitrine de mouton, mutton breast
poitrine de porc, pork belly
poitrine de veau, veal breast
poitrine fumée, slab of smoked bacon
poivrade, brown sauce of wine, vegetables, peppers and vinegar
poivre, pepper. *Au poivre* means w/peppercorns
poivre d'Ain, flavored *banon* (cheese)
poivre d'ane, bitter, peppery herb
poivre de cayenne, very hot red pepper
poivre de Chine, mouth-numbing type of peppercorn
poivre de la Jamaïque, allspice (the main ingredient of jerk
    seasoning)
poivre frais de Madagascar, green peppercorns
poivre mignonette, crushed peppercorns used on steaks
poivre noir, black peppercorns
poivre rose, pink peppercorns
poivre vert, green peppercorns
poivron, bell pepper
poivron doux, sweet bell pepper
poivron épicé, hot pepper
poivron rouge, red pepper
poivron vert, green pepper
polenta, corn meal/polenta (dish of
    boiled corn meal, w/butter and cheese)
Pomerol, a red wine (merlot) from Bordeaux
pommade, a thick paste
pomme, apple
pomme au four, potato baked in its skin   *au four*
pomme bonne femme, baked apple   *literally*
                                              "in the oven"

pomme de terre, potato
pomme de terre brayaude, oven-cooked potato
pomme en l'air, caramelized apple slices
    served w/blood sausage
pommes à l'anglaise, boiled potatoes
pommes allumettes, very thin french fries
pommes anna, sliced potato and cheese dish
pommes boulangère, a potato and
    meat dish/sliced potatoes w/onions
pommes château, potatoes fried in butter
pommes dauphine, potatoes mashed in
    butter and egg yolks, mixed in flour
    and deep fried

Most of the time pomme refers to potato though it means apple... sorry can't be more specific.

pommes dauphinoise, potatoes baked w/garlic, cheese and milk
pommes de terre à la berrichonne, herbed potatoes
pommes de terre à l'angoumois, potato and cabbage casserole
pommes duchesse, potatoes mashed in butter and egg yolks
pommes en robe de chambre, potatoes in their skin
pommes en robe des champs, potatoes in their skin
pommes fondantes, potatoes cooked in butter
pommes frites, french fries
pommes gratinées, potatoes baked w/cheese
pommes lyonnaises, potatoes sautéed w/onions
pommes mousseline, mashed potatoes
pommes nature, boiled or steamed potatoes
pommes nouvelles, new potatoes
pommes paille, fried strips of potatoes
pommes Pont-Neuf, french fries

Pommes frites, one of the miraculous joys of France.

pommes renversées, baked caramelized apple pudding
pommes sautées, fried potatoes
pommes soufflées, puffy slices of potatoes fried twice
pommes vapeur, steamed or boiled potatoes
pompe à l'huile, sweet flat bread flavored w/olive oil
pont l'évêque, strong, flavored, semi-hard cheese (usually
    served in square blocks)
porc, pork
porc au lait, pork cooked in milk
porc aux deux pommes, pork w/potatoes and apples
porc demi-sel, salted pork
porcelet, young suckling pig
porchetta/porketta, an Italian dish of roast, stuffed suckling pig

porc salé, salted pork
Porto, port
porto, au, w/port
port-salut/port du salut, mild, soft, buttery cheese
portugaises, a type of oyster
potable, drinkable
potage, soup (usually thick)
potage à la crème de coco, cream-of-coconut soup found in the
    French West Indies
potage au cerfeuil, soup of chervil and other herbs. A specialty
    in the Ardennes region of Belgium
potage bilbi, fish and oyster soup
potage bonne femme, potato and leek soup
potage cancalais, fish soup
potage Crécy, carrot soup
potage crème normande, cream of fish soup
potage cressonière, watercress soup
potage cultivateur, soup w/mixed vegetables and pork
potage d'Auvergne, lentil and potato soup
potage du Père Tranquille, lettuce soup
potage du Barry, cauliflower soup
potage Longchamp, soup featuring peas
potage nivernaise, carrot soup
potage parmentier, leek and potato soup
potage portugais, tomato *potage*
potage printanier, vegetable soup
potage Saint-Germain, split-pea soup
potage soissonnais, haricot-bean soup
potage velouté, creamy soup

potage.

pot-au-feu, stew of meat and vegetables
pot-de-crème, mousse or custard dessert
potée, boiled pork (or beef) w/cabbage
pothine de boeuf, beef braised w/*calvados*. The *pothine* is a
    cast-iron casserole in which this dish is cooked
potiron, pumpkin
Pouilly-Fuissé, dry white wine from Burgundy
poularde, capon/fatted chicken
poularde Sainte-Hélène, chicken w/dumplings
poule, hen
poule au pot, stewed chicken w/vegetables
poule au riz, hen served w/rice

poule d'Inde, turkey hen

poule faisane, pheasant

poule farcie en daube à la berrichonne, boned, stuffed chicken in jelly.

NOT crazy about jellied meat.

poulet, chicken

poulet basquaise, chicken w/sweet peppers and tomatoes ("Basque style")

poulet Biarritz, chicken in white wine

poulet chasseur, chicken usually w/mushrooms and white wine. This can also be chicken in tomato sauce

poulet.

poulet créole, chicken in a white sauce (often spicy) and served w/rice

poulet de Bresse, free-range, corn-fed chicken

poulet de grain, corn-fed chicken. Sold in shops with a special ring around its "foot" to prove they are authentic.

poulet de Saint-Astier, chicken stew

poulet fermier, free-range chicken

poulet Marengo, chicken cooked in white wine w/tomatoes, garlic, mushrooms and shallots. Said to be the chicken dish served to Napoleon after the battle of Marengo in 1800

poulet rôti, roast chicken

poulpe, octopus

poulpe.

pourboire, tip

pour/à emporter, to go/take out

pourpier, purslane (a green used in salads)

pousse-pierre, seaweed

poussin, spring chicken

praire, clam

praline, caramelized almonds

premier cru, denotes a high-quality wine

pré-salé, lambs that graze on salt meadows

pressé, fresh squeezed

presse, à la, pressed

pression, draft beer. *À la pression* means from the tap

primeur, early season or spring fruits and vegetables

Prince-de-Galles, stuffed w/*pâté*

printanière, à la, w/spring vegetables

prisuttu, cured ham from Corsica

prix, price

prix fixe, fixed price

prix net, service is included

profiteroles, little cream puffs filled w/ice cream and covered in chocolate sauce

Profiteroles ~ food of the gods.

provençale, à la, w/garlic, onions, herbs and tomatoes ("Provence style"). Provence is one of France's wine-growing regions and, of course, one of the world's best-known and loved tourist destinations

prune, plum

pruneau/pruneau sec, prune

pudding, custard/pudding

puits d'amour, pastry filled w/custard

pulenta, chestnut-flour bread from Corsica

purée, strained fruit or vegetables.
En purée means mashed

purée de pommes de terre, mashed potatoes

pyramide au chocolat, chocolate pyramid filled w/chocolate pieces and sauces, whipped cream and butter

quartiers d'orange glacés, caramelized orange sections. A dessert found on menus in Provence

quart, un, on a menu this denotes a quarter-liter of wine

quatre-épices, a blend of four spices (nutmeg, cloves, ginger and white pepper)

quatre-quarts, a cake made from four ingredients – eggs, flour, butter and sugar – of equal weight. A specialty in Brittany

quatre-quarts is like pound cake.

quenelle, dumpling

quenelles de foie de veau, calf's-liver dumplings. A specialty in Luxembourg

quetsche, small plum/liquor made from plums

queue, tail

queue de boeuf, oxtail

quiche, egg tart w/vegetable, seafood or meat filling

quiche au fromage blanc, bacon and white cheese *quiche*

quiche lorraine, *quiche* w/cheese, bacon and onions

râble, loin of rabbit

râble de lièvre, saddle of rabbit

racasse, scorpion fish

raclette, cheese heated until it begins to melt. The melted part is scraped off and placed on a warm plate to be eaten w/boiled potatoes, pickles and pickled onions. This can also refer to melted cheese on a *baguette*

radis, radish

radis noir, large black radish

ragoût, stewed/meat stew

raie, ray/skate (fish)

raifort, horseradish

raisin, grape(s)

raisins de Corinthe, currants

raisins de table, dessert grapes

raisin sec, raisin(s)

raïto, red wine, tomato and onion sauce

ramequin, small cheese tart or a small casserole

rancio, dessert wine

râpé, shredded/grated. *La râpée* is a creamed-potato pancake

rascasse, fish found in the Mediterranean (scorpion fish)

ratatouille, eggplant casserole

rave, root vegetable

ravigote, vinegar dressing (w/herbs and shallots)

ravioli, ravioli. Common in Nice and all of the French Riviera

reblochon, soft, strong cheese

refroidi, chilled

régional(e), from the region/local

reine, à la, w/mince meat or poultry

à la reine...
of the
queen.

reine-claude, small green or yellow plums (greengage)

reinette, fall and winter apple

religieuse, *éclair* pastry. This pastry got its name because it looks like a nun in her habit

rémoulade, mayonnaise sauce

renversée, turned out of its cooking container

repas, meal

Rhône, this valley is one of France's wine regions (located in South Central France) and known for its white and red wines

rhubarbe, rhubarb

rhum, rum

Ricard, anise-flavored aperitif

Richelieu, à la, w/tomatoes, bacon and potatoes

rigotte, goat cheese

rillettes, highly seasoned meat baked in its own fat (potted meat)

rillons, pork belly
ris, sweetbreads
ris d'agneau, lamb sweetbreads
ris de..., sweetbreads
ris de veau, veal sweetbreads (the pancreas of a veal calf)
rissole, pastry/meat or fish patty
rissolé, fried until brown and crisp
riz, rice. *Crème de riz* is rice flour
    (very finely gound rice)
riz à l'impératrice, rice pudding
riz basquais, spicy rice
riz complet, brown rice
rizotto, risotto
riz pilaf, rice boiled in bouillon w/onions (rice pilaf)
riz safrané, saffron rice
riz sauvage, wild rice
robe des champs, en, in its skin
Robert, a brown sauce w/onions, white wine and mustard
rocambole, a member of the onion family
rognon, kidney
rognonnade, veal loin
rognons blancs, testicles
rognons de veau à la liégeoise, roast veal kidneys
romarin, rosemary
romsteck, rump steak
rondelle, round slice
roquefort, blue cheese
roquette, arugula (rocket)
rosbif, roast beef
rosé, rosé. This can also refer to rare meat
rosette, dried sausage/small round piece
Rossini, a dish that includes *foie gras* and truffles
rôti, roast/roasted
rouelle, a slice cut at an angle
rouelle de veau, veal shank
rouge, red
rouget, red mullet
rouille, spicy sauce of peppers, garlic and tomatoes
rouilleuse, red garlic mayonnaise
roulade, rolled slice of meat or fish w/stuffing/"Swiss roll"
    dessert w/cream or jam stuffing

ris - ree
riz - ree
*Don't get
'em mixed
up.*

*Rognon ~
run yun*

*Pass on the
entire Rongum
selection*

Rouget.

roulé, rolled
rouleau, roll of...
roussillonnade, grilled sausage and mushroom dish
roux, flour and butter mixture (used to thicken sauces or soup)
rouzoles, crêpes filled w/bacon and ham
rumsteck, rump steak
sabayon, creamy dessert of wine, sugar, egg yolks and
    flavoring/cream wine sauce
sablé, shortbread cookie
saccharine, saccharin
sachet de thé, tea bag
safran, saffron
saignant, very rare
saindoux, pork fat
Saint-Amour, red wine from Beaujolais
Saint-Emilion, red wine form Bordeaux
Saint-Estèphe, red wine from Bordeaux
Saint-Germain, w/peas
Saint-Honoré, cake w/cream
Saint-Hubert, sauce w/bacon and chestnuts
Saint-Jacques, sea scallop
Saint-Julien, red wine from Bordeaux
Saint-Marcellin, goats' or cows' cheese w/a smoky flavor
Saint-Raphaël, quinine-flavored aperitif
Saint-Paulin, mild, semi-soft cheese
Saint-Pierre, John Dory fish (a firm-textured, white-fleshed fish
    w/a mild, sweet flavor and low fat content)
saison, season
salade, salad
salade antiboise, salad usually w/fish, capers and green peppers
salade au bleu, salad w/blue cheese (and frequently walnuts)
salade au chapon, salad served on toast rubbed w/garlic
salade aux noix, green salad w/walnuts
salade cauchoise, ham, potato and celery salad
salade chiffonnade, shredded lettuce and sorrel
salade composée, chef's salad
salade d'Auvergne, salad w/blue cheese dressing
salade de boulghour, bulgur wheat salad
salade de crudités, chopped vegetable salad
salade de fruits, fruit cocktail
salade de gésiers, green salad w/gizzards

St. Emilion – personal favorite.

Chapon refers to the toast.

salade de liège, bean and potato salad. A specialty in Belgium
salade de museau de boeuf, marinated beef headcheese
salade de saison, seasonal salad
salade de tomates, tomato salad
salade folle, mixed salad usually w/green beans

Salade folle ~ crazy salad

salade lyonnaise, *hors d'oeuvre* of seasoned meats in an oil, shallot and vinegar dressing
salade mélangée, mixed salad
salade mêlée, mixed salad
salade mesclun, mixed greens
salade mixte, mixed salad
salade multicolore, salad w/radishes, peppers, egg, cucumber, corn and basil
salade niçoise, salad usually w/tomatoes, anchovies or tuna, potatoes, vinegar and black olives (served as a main course)
salade panachée, mixed salad
salade paysanne, salad w/eggs and pieces of bacon
salade russe, diced vegetables in mayonnaise
salade simple, green salad
salade verte, green salad
salade wallonie, warm salad w/lettuce, bacon and fried potatoes. A specialty in Belgium
salaisons, an hors d'oeuvre of olives, anchovies and/or herring
salé, salted
salicorne, algae used as a condiment
salmis, roasted game or poultry
salpicon, stuffing w/sauce
salsifis, salsify (oyster plant)

Salpicon – like the word and the concept!

Sancerre, white and pale, light-bodied red wines from the Loire Valley
sandre, pike
sandwich, sandwich
sandwich au fromage, cheese sandwich
sandwich au jambon, ham sandwich
sandwich au saucisson, dried-sausage sandwich
sandwich aux rillettes, *pâté* sandwich
sandwich crudités, lettuce and/or chopped vegetable sandwich
sang, blood
sanglier, wild boar

Sanglier. A specialty in the Ardennes.

sans, without
sans arêtes, boneless
sans peau, skinless
sarcelle, teal (river duck)
sardine, sardine
sarrasin, buckwheat
sarriette, summer savory (an herb)
sartando, small fried fish w/hot vinegar
sartenais, hard, strong cheese from Corsica
sauce, sauce/gravy/salad dressing
sauce à la crème, cream sauce
sauce aurore, a white sauce w/tomato purée
sauce aux câpres, a white sauce w/capers
sauce bigarade, orange sauce
sauce bretonne, egg, butter and mustard sauce
sauce café de Paris, cream, mustard and herb sauce
sauce catalane, tomato, orange and garlic sauce
sauce gaillarde, seasoned mayonnaise
sauce mornay, cheese sauce
sauce poulette, mushroom, egg yolk and wine sauce
sauce soubise, onion sauce
sauce Suzette, orange sauce
sauce veloutée, creamy soup/white sauce (*roux* mixed w/poultry,
    fish, veal or mushroom stock)
sauce vinot, wine sauce
saucisse, sausage
saucisse à l'ail tiède, garlic sausage
    (served warm)
saucisse à la navarraise, sausage w/wine
    and sweet peppers
saucisse de Francfort, hot dog/frankfurter
saucisse de Strasbourg, beef sausage
saucisse de Toulouse, fresh pork sausage
saucisson, dried sausage
saucisson à l'alsacienne, poached sausage w/horseradish sauce
saucisson à la lyonnaise, poached sausage w/potato salad
saucisson chaud de Lyon en croûte, sausage w/cubes of fat
    and baked in pastry
saucisson de Lyon, dried seasoned sausage
sauge, sage
saumon, salmon

[handwritten margin notes:]
Saucisse ~ Sausage like bratwurst
Saucisson ~ Sausage like Salami
Sauge.

saumon de l'Atlantique, Atlantic salmon

saumon fumé, smoked salmon

Saumur-Champigny, light-bodied red wine from the
Loire Valley

saupiquet, spicy cream sauce w/bread crumbs

saupiquet des amognes, ham w/spicy cream sauce

sauté, sautéed

Sauternes, a fruity white dessert wine

sauvage, wild

Sauvignon de Touraine, white wine from the
Sauvignon Blanc grape

savarin, spongecake topped w/rum and cream

Savoie, one of France's wine-growing regions

savoyarde, flavored w/cheese. *À la savoyarde* also can refer to
a vermouth and cream sauce

scampi, prawns

scarole, escarole, a salad green (a type of *endive*)

scotch, scotch

sec, dry/straight

séché, dried

seiche, large squid/cuttlefish

seiches farcies, cuttlefish stuffed w/a mixture of sausage
and the meat of cuttlefish tentacles

seigle, rye

sel, salt

sel-épicé, salt spiced w/basil, nutmeg, cloves, cinnamon,
peppercorns, bay leaves and coriander

sel gemme, rock salt

sel gris, coarse rock or sea salt

selle, saddle of meat, generally the loin roast

selle anglaise, saddle of meat

sel marin, sea salt

selon arrivage, on a menu, this means the dish
depends on availability

selon grandeur/selon grosseur, price paid by the size or weight

sel raffiné, refined salt

semoule, semolina flour

sériole, amber jack, a type of fish

serpolet, wild thyme

serran, perch

service compris, service included

service non compris, service not include

serviette, napkin

s.g., abbreviation for price paid by the size or weight

sherry, sherry

sirop, syrup

sirop de sucre d'érable, maple syrup

smitane, cream, wine and onion sauce

socca, *crêpe* made w/chickpea flour served on the Côte d'Azur

soissons, white beans

soja, soy

sole, sole

sole normande, sole in a butter, onion, mushroom, white wine, cream and *calvados* sauce

son, bran

sorbet, sherbet

soubise, onion sauce

soubise-aurore, onion and tomato sauce

soucoupe, saucer

soufflé, soufflé (beaten egg whites w/various ingredients baked in a mold)

soufflé à la reine, soufflé w/poultry or meat

soufflé au Grand Marnier, soufflé w/orange liqueur

soufflé Rothschild, vanilla-flavored fruit soufflé

soupe, soup

soupe à l'oignon gratinée, French onion soup

soupe au pistou, vegetable and noodle soup (soup w/pesto found in the South of France)

soupe corse, Corsican soup of vegetables and herbs simmered w/a ham bone

soupe de montagne, Corsican soup of vegetables and herbs simmered w/a ham bone

soupe de poisson, fish soup

soupe paysanne, Corsican soup of vegetables and herbs simmered w/a ham bone

soupe pêcheur, fish soup

spaghetti, spaghetti

spats, small fish of the herring family

spécialité, specialty

spécialité de la maison, house specialty

spécialité du chef, chef's specialty

spécialités locales, local dishes

steak, steak

steak au poivre, steak topped w/crushed peppercorns. *Steak au poivre vert* is steak in a green-peppercorn sauce and *steak au poivre rouge* is steak in a red-peppercorn sauce

steak frites, steak and french fries

steak haché, hamburger

steak tartare, raw hamburger or chopped beef (usually topped w/a raw egg)

stockfish, niçoise spicy fish stew

stufatu, Corsican stew w/pasta

succès au pralin, meringue cake w/almonds

sucettes, lollipops ("suckers")

suchi, sushi

sucre, sugar

sucre candi, candy sugar

sucre de canne roux, brown sugar

sucre filé, spun sugar

Sucre filé is found adorning Croquembouche.

suprême, chicken-based sauce/breast of chicken or game or fillet of fish w/an unusual combination of ingredients

suprême de volaille, chicken breast. Usually a boned chicken breast in a creamy sauce

sur commande, to your special order

surgelé(s), frozen food

surlonge, beef chuck roast

sus, en, in addition. *Boisson en sus* means drink not included

Suze, an aperitif flavored w/gentian, an herb

tablier de sapeur, grilled breaded tripe

tagine/tajine, stew (lamb, veal or chicken) w/vegetables. This spicy stew is a specialty in North Africa (especially Morocco). Also a clay cooking vessel

Tagine.

tanche, the freshwater fish tench

tapenade, mixture of black olives, olive oil, lemon juice, capers and anchovies (a spread from Provence)

tarama, mullet-roe spread

tartare, chopped raw beef/in a salad, this refers to a mayonnaise-based sauce

Tanche.

tarte, pie/tart

tarte à l'oignon, onion and cream tart

tarte alsacienne, apple and custard tart

tarte au citron meringuée, lemon meringue pie

tarte au fruit, fruit tart

tartelette, small tart

tarte tatin, upside-down apple tart. Legend has it that this tart was "created" when the Tatin sisters (who operated a restaurant) put the tart in the oven and left for church. They discovered their mistake, turned it upside down and served it.

tarte tropézienne, yellow cake w/custard filling (created by a Polish baker in 1955 in St Tropez)

tartine, open-faced sandwich (half baguette w/butter)

tasse, cup

Tavel, rosé wine from the Côte du Rhône region

tendre, tender

tendre de tranche, round steak

tendron, breast

tendron de veau, veal breast

terrine, *pâté*/prepared in an earthenware dish

terrine de campagne, pork and liver *pâté*

terrine de légumes, ground and seasoned vegetable loaf

terrinée, caramel-rice pudding

tête, head

tête de veau vinaigrette, calf's head w/vinegar and oil dressing

teurgoule, caramel-rice pudding

thé, tea

thé au lait, tea w/milk

thé citron, tea w/ lemon

thé glacé, iced tea

thé nature, tea w/out milk

thon, tuna

thon mirabeau, tuna cooked in eggs and milk

thym, thyme

tian, a dish (usually rice, vegetables and cheese) cooked in an oval-shaped earthenware dish used on the Côte d'Azur

tian de Saint-Jacques et légumes provençal, sea scallops on a bed of chopped vegetables

tiède, lukewarm

tilleul, herb tea

timbale, cup. *En timbale* means meat, fish or fruit in a mold

ti punch, rum, lime and sugarcane syrup drink found in the French West Indies

The luscious-sounding Tartine buerré is Nothing more than buttered bread.

Not on your life !

Ti means petit

117

tisane, herbal tea

toast, toast (little pieces of crispy bread)

tomate, tomato. This also is the name for a drink of *pastis* mixed w/grenadine

tomates à la provençal, baked tomatoes stuffed w/bread crumbs, garlic and parsley

tomates concassées, roughly chopped tomatoes

tomates farcies, tomatoes stuffed w/seasoned bread crumbs

tomme (or tome) au marc, the crust of this smooth and creamy cheese is made of grape pulp. Also known as *fondu aux raisins*

tomme (de Savoie), soft, mild cheese

tonique, tonic

tonneaux en chêne, oak barrels

topinambour, Jerusalem artichoke

tortue, turtle

tortue véritable, turtle soup

toulousaine, usually means served w/sweetbreads or truffles ("Toulouse style")

tourain, bread and garlic soup

tourin bordelais, French onion soup (usually w/bread on the bottom of the bowl)

tournedos, round cut of prime steak

tournedos Rossini, *tournedos* served w/Madeira wine sauce and served w/*foie gras* and/or truffles

tourta da blea, Swiss chard pie

tourte, pie

tourteau, large crab

tourte aux blettes, sweet tart of eggs, cheese, raisins, pine nuts and chard

tourte du jour, savory pie of the day

tourtière, pastry filled w/prunes and/or apples. Also the name for a cooking dish

tourton, pastry filled w/prunes, apples, spinach and garlic

tout compris, everything is included in the price

tout épice, allspice

tranche, slice. *Tranché* means sliced

tranche grasse, sirloin tip

tranche napolitaine, slice of layered ice cream

travers de porc, spareribs

treipen, black pudding and sausages w/potatoes

très, very
trifle, trifle
tripe, tripe
tripe à la luxembourgeoise, tripe
specialty found in Luxembourg

Remember the general rule about Tripe... don't.

tripes à la mode, tripe in butter, onions and *calvados.*
A popular dish in Normandy
tripes à la mode de Caen, tripe baked w/calf's feet
tripes à la mode narbonnaise, tripe in tomato sauce
Triple Sec, orange liqueur
tripoux, mutton tripe
trompettes des morts, wild mushrooms
tronçon, large slice of meat or fish
trouchia, trout. In Provence, this refers to an omelet
truffat, potato-cream pie
truffe, truffle. *Truffé* means w/truffles. Truffles are extremely
expensive wild fungi that grow around the roots of trees.
They must be "sniffed out" by pigs or dogs. *Truffes* also
refers to chocolate truffles
truffettes dauphinoise, chocolate truffles
truite, trout
truite à l'ardennaise, Belgian dish of
trout cooked in a wine sauce
truite au bleu, poached trout

Truite.

truite meunière, trout in a parsley and butter sauce
truite saumonée, salmon trout
ttoro, Basque mixed-fish dish
tuile, almond cookie
turbon, ingredients cooked in a ring mold
turbot, turbot, a fish
turbotin, small turbot
vacherin, mellow Swiss cheese
vacherin glacée, baked meringue dessert
valençay, goat's-milk cheese
Vallée d'Ange, w/cooked apples and cream (named after a region
in Normandy)
vanille, vanilla
vanneau, small bird
vapeur, steamed
varié/variés, assorted
veau, veal

veau Marengo, veal w/garlic, tomatoes, white wine and cognac
végétarien/végétarienne, vegetarian
velouté, creamy soup/white sauce
(*roux* mixed w/poultry, fish,
veal or mushroom stock)
velouté d'asperges, creamy white asparagus soup
venaison, venison
ventre, stomach/belly
ventrèche, salted and seasoned pork belly
vénus, clam
verdures, green salad vegetables
verjus, the juice of unripened grapes
vermicelle, tiny, thin noodles used in soup
vermouth, vermouth
vernis, large clam
verre, glass
vert, green/a sauce of spinach,
mayonnaise and herbs
vert-pré, watercress garnish
verveine, the herbal tea lemon verbena
vessie, cooked in a pig's bladder
viande, meat
viande séchée, thin slices of cured beef
viandes froides, cold meats
vichy, w/glazed carrots
vichyssoise, cold leek and potato soup
vieille, old
vieille cure, wine-distilled liqueur
vieille prune, plum-based *eau-de-vie*
vierge beurre, a simple butter sauce w/lemon juice, salt and pepper
vierge huile d'olive, virgin olive oil
vieux, old
vigneronne, sauce w/grapes and wine
vigne, sarments de, vine cuttings used w/grilled foods
vin, wine
vinaigre, vinegar
vinaigre balsamique, balsamic vinegar
vinaigre de vin, wine vinegar
vinaigrette, generally a salad dressing
of vinegar, mustard, herbs and oil
vin blanc, white wine
vin chambré, wine served at room temperature

Verjus is sometimes used instead of vinegar.

Une verre de vin rouge

Vielle cure means remedy... An excuse to drink...

Vin is pronounced Van with just a hint of the 'N'.

vin cuit, sweet dessert wine
Vin Délimité de Qualité Supérieure (VDQS), denotes a local
    wine made according to strict standards
vin de maison, house wine
vin de paille, straw wine w/a strong flavor and aroma
vin de pays, wine guaranteed to originate in a certain region
    ("country wine")
vin de table, table wine
vin de xérès, sherry
vin doux, sweet wine/dessert wine
vin doux naturel, naturally sweet wine
vin du pays, local wine
vin gris, pink wine
vin jaune, a dry whiite wine from Jura
vin liquoreux, sweet wine
vin mousseux, sparkling wine
vin nouveau, new wine
vin ordinaire, table wine
vin rosé, rosé wine
vin rouge, red wine
vin sec, dry wine
violet de Provence, braid of garlic
violette, crystallized violet petals
vivant/vivante, alive/living
vodka, vodka
volaille, poultry
vol-au-vent, puff pastry filled w/fish, meat and/or sweetbreads
waterzooi, chicken or fish poached in a sauce w/vegetables. A
    Belgian specialty
waterzooi de poulet, chicken poached in a sauce w/vegetables
whisky, whisky
Williamine, a pear brandy
xérès, sherry
yaourt/yogourt, yogurt
Yvorne, a dry Swiss white wine
zeste, citrus zest
zeste de citron, lemon zest
zeste de citron confits, candied lemon zest
zeste d'orange, orange zest
zewelwai, onion and cream tart from Alsace

The French don't fill their glasses more than halfway

Volaille ~ Voe-Lie.

PLACES TO EAT AND DRINK
BY ARRONDISSEMENT
Descriptions of restaurants listed here can be found on the page number following each listing.

Paris Arrondissements

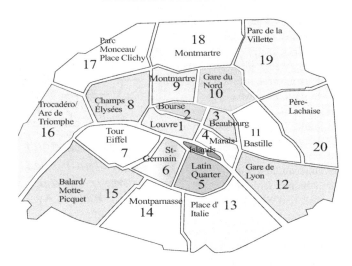

1. Louvre
Café Marly 45
Le Fumoir 23
Le Garde Robe 36
Le Grand Véfour 29
Juvenile's 24
Lavinia 40
Ô Chateau 41
Willi's Wine Bar 34
2. La Bourse
Le Art Source 35
Le Bourse et la Vie 21
Café Joueaux 44-45
Coinstot Vino 35
Frenchie 23
Le Grand Colbert 33
Legrand Filles et Fils 40
Aux Lyonnais 33
Osteria Ruggera 26

3. Beaubourg/Marais
Au Bascou 19
Bouillon République 20-21
Chez Janou 21
Le Hangar 24
Parcelles 26
Le Petit Marché 27
4. Marais/Ile-Saint-Louis
L'Ambroisie 29
L'Ange 20 19
Bistrot de L'Oulette 20
Bofinger 31
Café Beaubourg 44
Chez Marianne 32
Gaspard de la Nuit 24
Ma Bourgogne 33
Le Potager du Marais 43
Sorza 30
Le Trésor 36

18th Arrondissement:
Montmartre

R. Lambert

R. Bachelet

Rue Bachelet

Rue Clignancourt

Ramey

Rue Paul Albert

Rue Muller

Rue del Sarte

R. Picard

Rue Nodier

R. Livingston

Halle St-Pierre

R. Utrillo

Lamarck

Rue de la Barre

Rue Seveste Stairs

Anvers

Rue Ronsard

R. Steinkerque

Lamarck

Rue

Chevalier de la

Rue Dubois

Rue du

d'Orsel

Lamarck

Becbejer

Rue de la Bonne

Basilique du Sacré Coeur

FUNICULAIRE

Foyatier

R. Tardieu

Vincent

Rue

Rue

R. Azais

R. St. E

Rue Gabrielle

R. Chappe

R. Barsacq

Rue

Mont Cenis

R. Paul Feval

Saint

Musée du Vieux Montmartre

Rue Corrot

du

Rue

place du Tetre

R. Eleuthere

R. Drevet

Trois

R. Tardieu

Frères

Rue

Rue

Rue

St. Rustique

Norvins

Espace Dali

place du Calvaire

Berthe

des

Vieuville

Martrys

des Saules

Poulbot

Rue de l'Abreuvoir

Rue

Rue Garreau

Rue

Abbesses

Houdon

Rue

Dereure

Rue Girardon

Sq. Suzanne Buisson

18th

Rue

Lepic

d'Orchampt

Durantin

des

Abbesses

R. Piemonte

île de Guelma

Germain Pilon

Véron

Avenue Junot

Rue

Burq

Rue

Rue

Rue

du Midi

Rue

Tholozé

Platanes

Rue Coustou

Rue Dereure

Rue

Lepic

Rue Joseph de Maistre

Rue Lepic

R. Planquette

R. Constance

Cauchois

Rue

Rue

Musée de l'Erotisme

Clichy

Tourlaque

Rue

Moulin Rouge

place Blanche

Blanche

Rue Joseph de Maistre

Cimetière de Montmartre

Caulaincourt

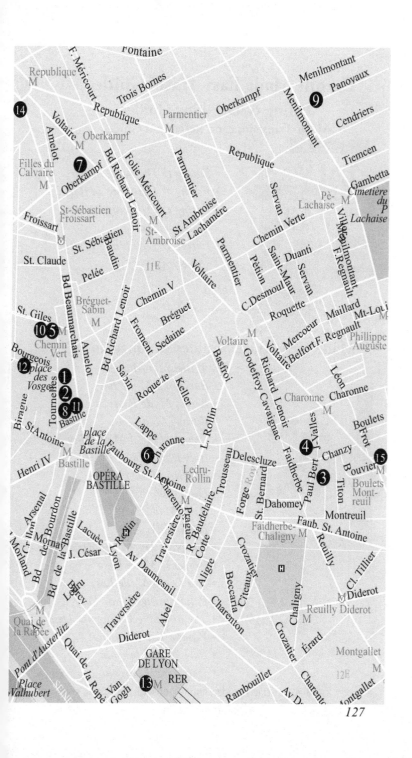

Europe Made Easy Travel Guides
Eating & Drinking Guides
Menu Translators and Restaurant Guides

- *Eating & Drinking in Paris*
- *Eating & Drinking in Italy*
- *Eating & Drinking in Spain and Portugal*
- *Eating & Drinking in Latin America*

Made Easy Travel Guides & Journals

- *Amsterdam Made Easy*
- *Barcelona Made Easy*
- *Berlin Made Easy*
- *Europe Made Easy*
- *French Riviera Made Easy*
- *Italy Made Easy*
- *Madrid Made Easy*
- *Oslo Made Easy*
- *Paris Made Easy*
- *Paris Walks*
- *The Next Time I See Paris*
- *Provence Made Easy*
- *San Diego Made Easy*
- *Palm Springs Made Easy*
- *The Amazing California Desert*
- *Europe Travel Journal*
- *Paris Travel Journal*
- *Italy Travel Journal*

For a list of all our travel guides, and to purchase our books, visit
www.eatndrink.com